WH...

CHINESE

LOVE SIGN

?

NEIL SOMERVILLE

Thorsons

Thorsons
An Imprint of HarperCollins*Publishers*
77–85 Fulham Palace Road,
Hammersmith, London W6 8JB

The Thorsons website address is: www.thorsons.com

Published by Thorsons 1995
This revised edition 1999

1 3 5 7 9 10 8 6 4 2

© Neil Somerville 1995, 1999

Neil Somerville asserts the moral right to
be identified as the author of this work

A catalogue record for this book
is available from the British Library

ISBN 0 7225 3938 X

Printed and bound in Great Britain by
Woolnough Bookbinding Ltd, Irthlingborough, Northamptonshire

CONTENTS

Use this table to find out the page number for your *Chinese love sign* combination

	RAT	OX	TIGER	RABBIT	DRAGON	SNAKE
RAT	4	6	8	10	12	14
OX	6	30	32	34	36	38
TIGER	8	32	54	56	58	60
RABBIT	10	34	56	76	78	80
DRAGON	12	36	58	78	96	98
SNAKE	14	38	60	80	98	114
HORSE	16	40	62	82	100	116
GOAT	18	42	64	84	104	118
MONKEY	20	44	66	86	104	120
ROOSTER	22	46	68	88	106	122
DOG	24	48	70	90	108	124
PIG	26	50	72	92	110	126

HORSE	GOAT	MONKEY	ROOSTER	DOG	PIG
16	18	20	22	24	26
40	42	44	46	48	50
62	64	66	68	70	72
82	84	86	88	90	92
100	102	104	106	108	110
116	118	120	122	124	126
130	132	134	136	138	140
132	144	146	148	150	152
134	146	156	158	160	162
136	148	158	166	168	170
138	150	160	168	174	176
140	152	162	170	176	180

INTRODUCTION

Chinese astrology has been practised for thousands of years. However, it is only recently that we in the West have been able to appreciate the wonders of this ancient art.

In Chinese astrology there are 12 different signs. Each sign is named after an animal and each animal sign rules a year. Those born in that year inherit some of the characteristics of the animal.

To avoid the thorny problem of how to refer to the signs I have opted to use the masculine gender, but unless otherwise stated 'he' covers both the male and female of the sign.

I believe that the 12 Chinese signs can teach us much about ourselves and our relations with those around us. I hope that you will find **Chinese Love Signs** informative and enjoyable reading.

THE RAT

Key characteristics:

Charming, sociable, resourceful, quick-witted,
ambitious, crafty.

In love:

Romantic, attentive, affectionate – and hard to resist.

The rat may not be considered the most endearing of creatures, but it is resourceful, intelligent and alert. As are those born under the first of the Chinese signs.

Governed by charm, he has a friendly, sociable manner and a good understanding of human nature. The Rat knows how to put others at ease and is invariably popular. A keen socializer, he enjoys attending parties and functions and has a good appreciation for the finer things in life. He can also be crafty, manipulative and driven by ambition.

2

He likes to keep himself continually busy and one of his main aims in life is to improve upon his present situation.

The Rat is a private individual and will not allow others to pry to closely into his own concerns. He likes to retain a certain independence in his actions. The Rat is a survivor and even when events go against him, he will often be the first to pick up the pieces and look for new challenges.

Being sociable, the Rat values relations with others and makes friends easily. He is supportive to his partner and will try to establish a close-knit family. He tends to have a large family and makes a loving and caring parent. With his wide interests and fertile imagination he will encourage his children but will also be a good disciplinarian.

The female Rat has a lively and outgoing manner, but no matter how successful or busy she might be, her family always comes first. The male Rat is confident and suave. But behind his personable air lurks a sharp mind.

The Rat is the first sign in the Chinese zodiac and, with his charm and outgoing manner, he is invariably popular and well-respected.

Famous Rats:

Lauren Bacall, Kenneth Branagh, Marlon Brando, Charlotte Bronte, Richard Nixon, William Shakespeare.

RAT AND RAT

General Relations

The Rat delights in the company of others and when it is another lively and sociable Rat, the two can have much fun together. Between them they have many interests they can share and, as both enjoy conversation, they may wile away many a happy hour locked in intense discussion.

When two Rats work together their combined skills can bring them considerable success. Both are enterprising and opportunistic, and both are keen to make the most out of their skills. Rats sometimes spread their energies too widely and become involved in more activites than they can sensibly handle. If they can control their restless and greedy natures, then a working relationship between them goes well.

In Love and Marriage

The attraction between two Rats is strong. Both are romantic and passionate and they have a good understanding of each other. Both delight in socializing, entertaining and travelling and may have a fondness for literature and the arts.

They place much value on their home life and, if they have children, make caring and protective parents. Rats value their family bonds and the Rat family is likely to be close knit. Although Rats can be indulgent, a Rat couple handles financial matters well and enjoy a good standard of living.

A Rat couple can find much happiness together but they would do well to maintain some separate interests rather than insist on complete togetherness. Also Rats can be forthright and highly critical and this may sometimes lead to acrimonious exchanges. However, as a couple they strive to overcome problems and make a devoted pair.

A good match

RAT AND OX

General Relations

Although the Rat and Ox have very different personalities – the Rat being far more outgoing then the Ox – these two signs get on well together. They trust and respect each other and can become firm friends. The Rat particularly appreciates the Ox's confident and steadfast nature, while the Ox delights in the vivacity and charm of the Rat. General relations between the Rat and Ox are often excellent.

The Rat and Ox also work well together. The Rat is the master of PR and customer relations while the Ox provides method, order and consistency. They recognize and capitalize on each other's strengths and there is a great deal of trust and respect between them. Together they can build up an excellent working relationship.

In Love and Marriage

There is a strong attraction between the Rat and the Ox and, in love and marriage, they can find much happiness. The character differences that exist between them often prove complementary and each loves and admires the other dearly.

The Rat is the more outgoing of the two and the Ox gains from the Rat's vivacity, love of life and sociable nature. Under the Rat's influence the Ox may become more outgoing and more at ease in his relations with others. Similarly, the Rat admires the Ox's loyalty, strength of character and ambition. The Rat feels reassured by having such a resolute and reliable partner. Both attach much importance to their home and, if they have children, make caring and conscientious parents.

The Rat and the Ox also seek stability and security in their lives and with the Rat's thrift and the Ox's careful nature, most Rat-Ox couples are materially well off.

An excellent match

RAT AND TIGER

General Relations

The Rat and Tiger are two lively and outgoing signs and they generally get on well together. Both are keen socializers and, with their wide interests, they invariably have interests they can share. The Tiger is very much taken with the Rat's charm and personable manner while the Rat enjoys the Tiger's vibrant, enthusiastic and confident personality.

When the Rat and Tiger work together each is quick to appreciate the strengths of the other. The Rat values the Tiger's enterprise and enthusiasm, while the Tiger recognizes the Rat's resourcefulness and ability to spot opportunities. Both are ambitious and both are capable of devising many wonderful and innovative ideas.

In Love and Marriage

The Rat and the Tiger are often attracted to each other. Both have lively and sociable natures and they enjoy each other's company. They are also both highly passionate signs and the physical attraction between them is strong.

The Tiger delights in the Rat's charming and sociable manner as well as appreciating his skills as a homemaker. The Rat, in turn, finds reassurance in the Tiger's confident and ebullient manner.

However, their different attitudes to money may cause problems. The Tiger tends to be generous in his spending while the Rat is more thrifty. In addition, the Rat feels unsettled by the Tiger's restless nature and he must accept that the Tiger needs a degree of independence. Both are frank in expressing their views and this may give rise to some heated exchanges.

Their relationship may not always be harmonious, but there is much love and passion between them.

A reasonably good match

RAT AND RABBIT

General Relations

Although the Rat and the Rabbit are both sociable signs neither cares much for the other. The Rabbit, who has a calm and tranquil manner, feels ill at ease with the active and energetic Rat, while the Rat considers the Rabbit reserved and over-sensitive. They may delight in a once-in-a-while conversation but rarely do the two signs become close friends.

When the Rat and Rabbit work together, however, their different skills may prove complementary. The Rabbit appreciates the Rat's skills at seeking out opportunities as well as his outgoing and action-oriented character. The Rat values the Rabbit's organizational and commercial skills and shrewd judgement. Nevertheless, due to their different peronalities, they may not always feel completely at ease working together.

In Love and Marriage

The Rat and the Rabbit are two passionate and sensual signs and there may be a strong physical attraction between them. Both are charming and sociable, are homelovers and enjoy literature and the arts. The early stages of their relationship may bring much happiness, but the longer they know each other, the more difficult their relationship may become. Their temperaments are ill suited and, in love and marriage, a match between them may prove challenging.

The Rat is an active and energetic sign and tends to involve himself in a multitude of activities and interests. The Rabbit, however, seeks a much quieter and more settled lifestyle. The Rat may find the cautious nature of the Rabbit a restrictive influence while the Rabbit may find him brash and overbearing.

A difficult match

RAT AND DRAGON

General Relations

The Rat and the Dragon get on extremely well together. They are both lively, outgoing and sociable signs and they enjoy each other's company. They have many interests in common and there is a great deal of trust and understanding between them. The Rat and Dragon may often become close and lifelong friends.

When the Rat and Dragon work together they can enjoy considerable success. Both are ambitious, entertaining and work hard, and each values the skills of the other. The Dragon, in particular, appreciates the Rat's ability to seek out new opportunities and his skills at PR, while the Rat values the Dragon's resolute and confident manner. They trust and support each other and in business make a formidable and successful team.

In Love and Marriage

This is a splendid match and in love and marriage the Rat and Dragon can find much happiness.

The Rat greatly admires the confident, determined and honourable nature of the Dragon and finds the Dragon lively and enjoyable company. Similarly, the Dragon loves the charm and sociable nature of the Rat as well as appreciating the Rat's resourcefulness and versatility.

They love each other dearly and, as both have passionate and sensual natures, the physical attraction between them is strong – together the Rat and Dragon have much fun. Both are also keen socializers and take great pleasure in entertaining and travel. They value their home life and, if they have children, make caring and attentive parents.

An excellent match

RAT AND SNAKE

General Relations

The Rat and Snake like and respect each other and general relations between them are often good. The Rat has many interests, a lively repartee and a charm that the Snake finds irresistible. The Rat in turn admires the Snake's calm, collected and thoughtful nature. They enjoy each other's company and while their tastes may not always converge – the Rat is much more a partygoer and socializer than the Snake – these two signs always have time for each other.

In business matters the Rat and Snake work well together. The Snake is the planner, organizer and adviser while the more action-orientated Rat sets plans into motion. The Snake also happily leaves the persuasive Rat to win over their customers but at the same time is a useful curb on some of the Rat's more risky notions. Both are ambitious, opportunist and materialistic.

In Love and Marriage

The attraction between these signs is strong. The Rat is captivated by the Snake's quiet and seductive charm, while the Snake is drawn to the Rat's warm, friendly and sensual nature. There is a powerful sexual charm between these two signs.

The two signs have similar outlooks; both are opportunists and both go through life intent on making the best of their abilities and skills. Both enjoy the material comforts in life and each aims for a high level of security. They are imaginative, enjoy intelligent discussion and may share a fondness for literature and the arts. They make caring and attentive parents and happily devote much time and energy to the upbringing of any children they have.

However, there are certain elements in their personalities that may cause problems. The Snake prefers to conduct his activities in a calm and measured way and may not always appreciate the Rat's more aggressive and blustering style. Similarly, the Rat may feel restricted by the Snake's possessive nature.

A good match

RAT AND HORSE

General Relations

The Rat and Horse are both outgoing signs and for a short time may find each other interesting company. However, their different temperaments may bring them into conflict and it is rare for the Rat and the Horse to become lasting friends. Both signs can be strong willed, opinionated and forthright in their views and this may lead to clashes between them. There is not much empathy between them and general relations between these two signs are poor.

Problems also emerge when the Rat and Horse work together, each wants to take the lead and dominate. There is mistrust between them; the Horse comes to view the Rat as conniving and thrifty, while the Rat sees the Horse as impulsive, impatient and short-tempered. There is little agreement between them and their competitive and independent spirits get the better of them – not a happy or successful arrangement.

In Love and Marriage

Both the Rat and Horse are romantic and passionate and they may fall deeply in love with each other. The Horse is seduced by the Rat's irresistable charm and the Rat by the Horse's lively and engaging manner. In the early stages of their relationship they have much fun.

However, relations between them quickly degenerate. Both the Rat and Horse are strong-willed and opinionated signs. Both are egoists and both want to dominate the relationship. The Rat is open and forthright in expressing his views and has little trouble in igniting the Horse's short temper.

Differing attitudes towards money may also cause problems. The thrifty Rat likes to keep a close control over the purse strings and views the Horse as a spendthrift and over-generous, while the Horse considers the Rat materialistic and tight-fisted.

A turbulent relationship

RAT AND GOAT

General Relations

Both the Rat and Goat know how to enjoy themselves and have a fondness for the good life. Together they enjoy wining, dining and leading an active social life. For the short to medium term the Rat and Goat can become good friends but each has traits which irritate the other and in time they may drift apart.

The Rat and Goat do not work well together. The Rat is a supreme opportunist, constantly geared up for action and determined to make the most of his abilities. He is competitive and ambitious. The Goat, however, needs to feel inspired and encouraged by others. The Rat is a self-starter, the Goat needs to be prodded. In work they are best going their separate ways.

In Love and Marriage

The Rat and Goat are both friendly and sociable signs and are often attracted to each other. Both possess romantic and passionate natures and both exude a strong sex appeal.

However, a relationship is hard to maintain and the longer-term prospects for a match between the Rat and Goat are decidedly bleak. As the intensity of their feelings begins to fade they begin to discover the gulf that exists between them.

The Rat is hardworking, industrious and energetic, while the Goat sets about his activities in a more leisurely manner. The Rat is thrifty while the Goat is a spendthrift. The Rat can be forthright and candid in his views, while the Goat is sensitive, shrinks from arguments and takes the Rat's criticisms very much to heart. The Rat has little time for the Goat's artistic and sometimes whimsical nature, and in turn, the Goat may come to view the Rat as greedy, meddlesome and fussy.

A difficult relationship

RAT AND MONKEY

General Relations

With their lively and sociable natures, the Rat and Monkey get on well together. Each greatly admires the other and with their great sense of fun they relate well to each other. The Rat delights in the Monkey's resourcefulness, wit and keen intellect while the Monkey enjoys the Rat's charm, drive and ambition. They may become close and lasting friends.

These two signs also work well together. Both are cunning, opportunist and determined to succeed; both recognize this drive and commitment in the other. However both the Rat and the Monkey can be crafty and they may be tempted to outwit the other; neither would succeed, as both are masters in the art of self-preservation. If they can both keep their attention firmly on their joint objectives, they could enjoy considerable success.

In Love and Marriage

The attraction between a Rat and Monkey is strong and in love and marriage they can find much happiness. With their many mutual interests and similar outlooks they are well matched and make a close and loving couple.

Both are keen socializers and between them have many friends. They take great pleasure in entertaining at home. Rats and Monkeys like to live well and, with their money-making talents, most Rat-Monkey couples are financially secure.

The Monkey appreciates the Rat for his loyalty, judgement, enthusiasm and skills as a homemaker. The Rat, in turn, delights in the Monkey's lively nature, quick wit, resourcefulness and enterprise. Although the Rat is more home orientated than the Monkey, together they devote much time and energy to their home and to any children they have. Also – as both have a good sense of humour – there is a strong element of fun in their relationship.

An excellent match

RAT AND ROOSTER

General Relations

Although the Rat and Rooster are two sociable and outgoing signs they do not relate well to each other. The Rat dislikes the vanity and egoism of the Rooster, while the Rooster finds the Rat too opportunist and manipulative. Neither places much trust in the other. Both signs can be notoriously blunt in their views and their outspokenness may prove the deathknell for any friendship that might have existed between them.

The Rat and the Rooster do not work well together. The Rooster plans his activities to the finest detail and is highly organized, while the Rat is supreme at taking advantage of a situation and places great reliance on his charm and resourcefulness. The Rat finds the Rooster too much of a restraining influence, while the Rooster dislikes the opportunistic ways of the Rat. They are not a successful combination.

In Love and Marriage

Initially there may be a strong attraction between them. Both like to lead an active social life, are keen partygoers and both have a deep love of conversation. In the early stages of their relationship they may have much fun together, each charmed by the qualities of the other. However, the longer-term prospects are difficult and each sign needs to make major adjustments if they want to remain together.

Although they may share similar interests, their different personality traits may bring them into conflict. Both are forceful characters, with minds of their own, and each may try to dominate the relationship. The Rooster is precise, orderly and well organized; the Rat prefers to live day to day. There is likely to be much arguing and bickering and, with their forthright natures, each may be critical of the other.

A turbulent match

RAT AND DOG

General Relations

The Rat and the Dog enjoy each other's company and may become reasonably good friends. The Rat admires the loyal and trusting nature of the Dog, while the Dog enjoys the sociable and outgoing ways of the Rat. Together they may pass many a happy hour socializing and exchanging views.

When the Rat and Dog work together they may not always be in full agreement but they may still benefit from each other's individual strengths. The Dog is not as materialistic as the Rat and the Dog may feel uneasy with the Rat's opportunistic ways. Similarly the thrifty Rat may despair of the Dog's spendthrift tendency. However, if they can reconcile their differences, the Dog can gain from the Rat's confident and enterprising nature, while the Dog can bring order, method and discipline to the Rat's ways of working.

In Love and Marriage

The Rat and Dog both possess qualities that the other admires and in love and marriage they can form a satisfactory relationship. The Rat greatly admires the loyalty and dependability of the Dog. He is mindful of the Dog's advice and the Dog is a useful curb on his impulsive nature. The Dog, in turn, delights in the Rat's charming, sociable and loving nature. The resourceful Rat instils confidence in the Dog and does much to alleviate some of his worries and anxieties.

They are both romantic and passionate signs and attach much importance to their home. They each strive to make their home comfortable, and with their strong family ties, it is likely to be full of family heirlooms, mementos of childhood and other items of nostalgia.

However, problems may arise. The Rat is thrifty and careful with his money, while the Dog, in the Rat's eyes, is over-generous. The Rat can be restless and enjoys change and challenges, while the Dog appreciates consistency and careful planning.

If they can reconcile their differences then the Rat and Dog can enjoy a content and fulfilling relationship.

RAT AND PIG

General Relations

The Rat and Pig have many interests in common and often become close and loyal friends. They are both outgoing, like socializing and have a fondness for the good things in life. They enjoy each other's company and often share similar viewpoints. General relations between these two signs are often excellent.

As colleagues or business partners, they can enjoy much success. Both work hard and diligently and both have entrepreneurial flair. The Pig delights in the Rat's skill in seeking out opportunities and developing ideas, while the Rat appreciates the Pig's commercial acumen and ability to make money. Providing the Rat does not try to take advantage of the Pig's trusting nature, they make a successful and formidable partnership.

In Love and Marriage

There is considerable attraction between the Rat and Pig and, in love and marriage, they can find happiness. Both are passionate and sensual signs and there is a strong physical attraction between them.

The Rat and Pig are home-oriented signs and attach much importance to their home and family. They make caring and attentive parents and devote much time and energy into creating and maintaining their home; between them they make sure it is tastefully furnished. Their home may, however, quickly become full; with the Pig's indulgence and the Rat's acquisitive and hoarding nature, they could have more possessions than they know what to do with.

Between them the Rat and Pig have considerable earning ability; most Rat and Pig couples are financially secure and are able to enjoy a good standard of living.

An excellent match

THE OX

Key characteristics:

Resolute, strong willed, ambitious, careful, patient, stubborn.

In love:

Loyal, caring and dependable.

Whether ploughing a field or pulling a cart, the ox is a strong and disciplined worker. The second of the Chinese signs is governed by equilibrium and tenacity and has a calm, quiet and orderly manner. While he may appear reserved, he is both resolute and tenacious.

The Ox sets about life in a cautious and methodical way. He plans his activities carefully and does not like change or anything too gimmicky or innovative. The Ox is a down-to-earth sort of person and while he may some-times lack tact, at least those who come in contact with him know exactly where he stands.

The Ox is methodical, diligent and often a loner. He likes to conduct his activities in his own way and to his own exacting standards. The Ox also prefers to specialize and have set interests rather than engage in a wide variety of activities.

The lady Ox is a practical person. She is keenly aware of her responsibilities and is supportive to her partner and her children. She also takes much delight in maintaining her home and others often marvel at her capabilities.

The male Ox is quiet but confident in his manner. He may not be as outgoing as other signs, but he has a sharp mind and a steely resolve.

However, the Ox does have his weaknesses. He can be stubborn and intransigent and does not adapt well to change. He can be prejudiced, inflexible and intolerant, he also has an awesome temper, although fortunately it is only used on rare occasions.

Famous Oxen

Johann Sebastian Bach, Charlie Chaplin, Dustin Hoffman, Anthony Hopkins, Napoleon, the late Princess of Wales.

OX AND OX

General Relations

There is respect and admiration between two Oxen but not always close friendship. Oxen are resolute, ambitious and often loners and while one Ox may recognize the qualities and tenacity in another Ox, they often prefer to keep their distance. Each Ox cherishes his independence and each likes to have his own way.

Both are hard and tenacious workers and if united by a common goal their perseverance and determination is invariably rewarded. In a working relationship between two Oxen it might be best if there is a clear division of responsibilities, otherwise there may be a tussle for authority. However, their ambitious and strong-willed natures can make them a powerful force.

In Love and Marriage

Oxen like secure, stable and calm lifestyles. As they have many common interests – and a mutual dislike of change – they may find a certain contentment together. As a couple they will conduct their activities in an orderly and efficient manner and as neither have expensive tastes most Ox couples are materially well off. Both also have practical natures and an Ox couple take much delight in creating and maintaining their home.

Oxen are loyal and faithful and keenly aware of their responsibilities, and as a couple there will be a great deal of trust between them. If Oxen have children they make conscientious, caring – but also strict – parents.

However, problems will arise. Both are strong-willed and stubborn so compromise may be difficult. As Oxen tend to be set in their ways, the relationship may be devoid of excitement or sparkle.

A good match

OX AND TIGER

General Relations

The Ox and Tiger are two forceful and determined signs and their personalities and temperaments simply clash. Neither finds it easy to relate to the other and general relations between them are poor. The practical and down-to-earth Ox finds the Tiger restless and volatile, while the Tiger views the Ox as unadventurous and intractable.

The differences in personality are also evident when they work together. The Tiger, often bubbling with enthusiasm and new ideas, finds the cautious Ox far too much of a restraining and inhibiting influence, while the Ox considers the Tiger rash, reckless and impulsive. Both signs clash and are likely to go their separate ways.

In Love and Marriage

A match between these two signs may prove both difficult and challenging.

Although there maybe initial attraction between the Ox and the Rabbit, a relationship will be difficult to maintain. The Ox prefers to set about his activities in a calm, methodical and orderly manner, while the Tiger is far more adventurous and outgoing. He revels in challenges and new situations and indulges in a wide range of activities. The Ox and Tiger live life at different speeds and in different ways.

The two signs have few interests in common. The Tiger likes to lead an active social life, while the Ox is not a great socializer. The Tiger is passionate and seeks fun and – while the Ox too enjoys life in his own way – he tends not to be as outgoing as the Tiger and is far more serious and restrained.

A difficult match

OX AND RABBIT

General Relations

The Ox and Rabbit admire each other and can become firm and loyal friends. Both prefer the quieter things in life and have many interests they can share. They relate well to each other and there is a good level of trust and understanding between them.

Both are methodical, diligent and conscientious workers and they like to plan their activities carefully. In a business relationship each benefits from the other. The Rabbit values the strength, tenacity and resolution of the Ox, while the Ox appreciates the shrewd business sense and commercial acumen of the Rabbit. They trust and support each other well. Admittedly neither are big risk-takers and both are conservative in outlook, but their joint skills usually bring them much success.

In Love and Marriage

There is considerable attraction between the Ox and Rabbit and in love and marriage they can find much happiness.

Although there are many personality differences between them – the Ox being more assertive than the Rabbit – they complement each other well. The Rabbit delights in having such a resolute, dependable and protective partner, while the Ox values the thoughtful, intelligent and affectionate ways of the Rabbit. Both signs are quiet and peaceloving and neither wants to pursue a particularly frenzied or volatile lifestyle. They both value their home life and are most supportive and attentive to each other. Together they appreciate music, literature and the arts and may have a fondness for the countryside.

With their methodical and conscientious natures – they each have the skill to earn a great deal – most Ox-Rabbit couples are materially well off.

An ideal match

OX AND DRAGON

General Relations

Although the Ox and Dragon may admire and respect each other they rarely become close friends. The Dragon is an extrovert, always active and a keen socializer. The Ox is quieter, more of a loner and lives life at a totally different speed to the Dragon. They have few interests in common and each prefers spending time with those more in tune with his own interests and personalities.

Relations between the Ox and Dragon improve when they work together. Both are ambitious and diligent workers and each recognizes the qualities in the other. The Ox values the enterprise and enthusiasm of the Dragon, while the Dragon appreciates the tenacity and persistence of the Ox. When united by a common objective the Ox and Dragon make a formidable team.

In Love and Marriage

The Ox and Dragon each have qualities that the other admires and for a time they may be attracted to each other. Each enjoys being with an opposite – an introvert exploring the world of an extrovert and vice versa.

However, despite any initial attraction between the Ox and Dragon, the long-term prospects for their relationship are difficult.

Both the Ox and Dragon are forceful characters and each may try to dominate the relationship. They can also both be stubborn and their forthright natures may lead to many heated exchanges. The Dragon likes to lead an active social life and engages in a wide variety of activities, while the Ox prefers a much gentler existence and prefers spending time quietly at home. The Dragon may feel restricted by the Ox, while the Ox may be unsettled by the restlessness of the Dragon.

A difficult match

OX AND SNAKE

General Relations

Thes Ox and Snake have much in common and general relations between them are good. Both have quiet and reserved natures and feel comfortable in each other's company. There is trust and understanding between them and they relate well to each other. The Ox admires the Snake's thoughtful and reflective ways, while the Snake values the Ox's caring, confident and determined nature.

The Ox and Snake also work well together. Both are ambitious and keen to make the most of their considerable talents. The Snake in particular values the tenacity, willpower and determination of the Ox, while the Ox values the Snake's keen business sense and original ideas. They trust and respect each other and as colleagues make a successful combination.

In Love and Marriage

These two signs are often attracted to each other and in love and marriage they make a good match.

The Ox greatly admires the Snake's discreet and thoughtful manner, cultivated tastes and good humour; and is captivated by his magnetic charm.

The Snake values the Ox's practical and dependable nature. The Ox is hard working, resolute and ambitious. He knows what he wants in life and such an attitude finds favour with an equally ambitious Snake.

The Ox is a splendid homemaker and quite often the Snake prefers to leave the decisions and domestic arrangements in the capable hands of the Ox, while he takes charge of their joint finances and paperwork. They work very much as a team.

Both may have an appreciation of the arts – particularly music and literature – and also outdoor activities.If they have a family, they make caring and responsible parents.

An excellent and fulfilling match

OX AND HORSE

General Relations

The Ox and Horse are two strong-willed and resolute signs; relations between them will be difficult. The Horse likes to lead an active and energetic lifestyle and is a keen socializer, while the Ox is quieter, more reserved and seeks a stabler existence.

Although the Ox and Horse may both be industrious and work hard, they do not work well together. The Ox is careful, methodical and cautious, while the Horse is far more adventurous and enterprising. Their resolute natures and different outlooks could lead to many disagreements between them – they are likely to go their own way and rely on their own methods rather than co-operate or work closely together.

In Love and Marriage

The Ox and Horse have few interests in common and pre-fer to set about their activities in different ways. Although it is possible that despite their many differences they may be attracted by the strengths and qualities of the other – the Ox may enjoy the wit, intelligence and affection of the Horse, while the Horse admires the integrity and loyalty of the Ox – in love they need to overcome many obstacles if they are to form a lasting and harmonious relationship.

Both the Ox and Horse can be strong-willed. Each may try to dominate and, given their stubborn natures, they may not always find it easy to compromise. The two signs live life at different speeds. The Horse likes to keep himself active, while the Ox prefers a quieter existence. The Horse is a romantic and may not find the Ox as passionate or affectionate as he would like.

A difficult match

OX AND GOAT

General Relations

The Ox and Goat have little in common. The hard-working and dutiful Ox has little appreciation of the Goat's imaginative, whimsical and often carefree nature. The Goat in turn finds the Ox too serious and matter-of-fact. The two signs rarely become friends.

The Ox is a hard and diligent worker and he sets about his activities with considerable determination and willpower. The Goat, however, does not have the tenacity or the ambition of the Ox and, while the Goat may admire the Ox's commitment, there is little understanding between them. The Ox despairs of the Goat's hesitant and indecisive nature, while the Goat finds the Ox intransigent and obstinate. In a working situation their personalities clash.

In Love and Marriage

In many ways the Ox and Goat are opposites. The Ox is careful, dutiful and methodical in his attitude, while the Goat is more easygoing. The Goat lives for the moment and is capricious, while the Ox is decisive and plans his activities with care.

The Ox does not fully appreciate the Goat's artistic and imaginative nature, while the more sensitive Goat feels ill at ease with the Ox's forthright manner. In addition, the Ox is careful with money, while the Goat tends to spend his freely.

There is a wide gulf between the signs and it takes an exceptional couple to make this relationship work.

A difficult match

OX AND MONKEY

General Relations

The Ox and Monkey have a mutual respect for each other. Although on a purely social level each may prefer signs more like themselves – the Monkey has a lively and outgoing nature while the Ox is quieter – both recognize qualities in the other and, for the most part, can get on well together without necessarily becoming close friends.

The Ox and Monkey work successfully as a team. The Ox values the Monkey's resourcefulness and quick thinking, while the Monkey gains much from the Ox's more practical and persistent approach. The more cautious Ox also acts as a stabilizing influence on the Monkey, while in turn the Ox benefits from the Monkey's inventiveness. Both signs are ambitious and astute. They have a good respect and regard for each other.

In Love and Marriage

For all their many differences, the Ox and Monkey are often attracted to each other and in love and marriage they can make a good match.

The Ox has the discipline and tenacity that the Monkey often lacks and can be a steadying influence. The Ox gives the Monkey a sense of security and stability as well as being loyal and dependable. The Monkey makes lively and enjoyable company and this can be a tonic for the quiet and dutiful Ox. He may also become more outgoing under the Monkey's influence. The Monkey shows the Ox how to enjoy life rather than to wrap himself up in his own individual concerns and activities.

If they have children, both make caring and conscientious parents and the children benefit from the different qualities found in an introvert and extrovert parent.

A good match

OX AND ROOSTER

General Relations

These two signs get on well together and can become firm friends. The Rooster admires the determined, calm and sincere manner of the Ox, while the Ox finds the Rooster – with his many interests and outgoing nature – stimulating company.

The Ox and Rooster also work well together, either as colleagues or business partners. Each motivates and encourages the other. The Ox gains from the Rooster's organizational talents and more outgoing nature, while the Rooster is inspired by the Ox's tenacity and willpower; both are efficient and methodical in their duties.

In Love and Marriage

The Ox and Rooster are often attracted to each other and are ideally suited. They share similar values and outlooks and they complement each other extremely well.

Together they spend much time on their joint interests; both may be keen gardeners and enjoy the countryside and nature as well as being avid readers. They also devote considerable energy to their home and to any children that they have. Both make conscientious parents.

The Rooster helps to make the Ox more outgoing as well as broadening his interests, while the Ox is a steadying influence on the Rooster's sometimes volatile nature. Both are conservative in outlook, and keen to make the most of their considerable abilities.

In love and marriage the signs can form a lasting relationship founded on love, loyalty and trust.

An excellent relationship

OX AND DOG

General Relations

Although the Ox and Dog may admire each other's open, sincere and dependable natures their outlooks and personalities often clash. The Ox's domineering attitude may be resented by the Dog, while the Dog's idealism is not fully appreciated by the Ox.

Similarly when the Ox and Dog work together relations prove difficult. The Ox is ambitious, tenacious and eager to give his best. He has little patience with the Dog's worrying and sometimes pessimistic tendencies. The Ox does not share the Dog's idealism or approve of his generous and spendthrift ways. The Dog, in turn, may resent the Ox's authoritarian and intransigent attitude. In work there will be a lack of trust and understanding between them.

In Love and Marriage

In love and marriage this is a challenging, but not impossible, match.

Both these signs share an important quality: loyalty; and both are faithful to their partner. The Dog admires the confident and determined nature of the Ox and appreciates his sincere and dependable manner. Similarly, the Ox values the affection, support and discretion of the Dog.

The practical and down-to-earth Ox may not always be as spontaneous as the Dog may like. However if the Ox and the Dog are prepared to make the effort it is possible that they can form a meaningful relationship. The anxious Dog may benefit from the Ox's confident manner, while the Dog may help the Ox broaden his interests and make him more sociable. Both attach great importance to their home life, and they will pour much time and energy into any children.

A challenging – but rewarding – relationship

OX AND PIG

General Relations

There is much respect between the Ox and Pig and these two signs can become firm friends. The Ox likes the sincerity and openness of the Pig, while the Pig admires the integrity and dutiful nature of the Ox. Although the Ox may not be such a keen socializer as the Pig, they do share many interests and both may have a particular interest in gardening, the countryside and outdoor life.

The Ox and Pig also work well together. Both are persistent and diligent workers and once committed to a certain objective they work long and hard to achieve their goal. They are patient and tenacious and there is much respect and loyalty between them. The Ox gains from the Pig's enterprise and the Pig from the Ox's methodical manner – together they will succeed.

In Love and Marriage

The Ox and Pig are often attracted to each other and together can build a successful relationship.

Both the Ox and Pig are open and honest in their feelings and there is considerable trust between them. They are both hard-working and conscientious and between them they enjoy a stable and comfortable way of life. They both value their home, have practical natures and are constantly active. They also have a fondness for the outdoor life and can be keen gardeners or ramblers. The main difference between them, however, is that the Pig enjoys a much more active social life than the Ox and there are times when the Pig may wish the Ox were more outgoing.

An excellent match

THE TIGER

Key characteristics:

Assertive, adventurous, independent, inventive, generous, restless and impulsive.

In love:

Sincere, passionate and a true romantic!

Proud, distinctive and ever alert, the tiger is a majestic animal. Those born under the third of the Chinese signs are bold, enterprising and have little trouble in gaining the respect of others.

The Tiger has a lively nature. He likes to keep himself active and often has a wide range of interests. He follows the courage of his convictions and many admire him for his sincere and courageous manner. The Tiger is open in expressing his views and cannot tolerate falsehood or hypocrisy. He holds firm opinions and while he might dispense advice to others, he rarely listens to that given to him, preferring to rely on his own instinct and intuition. With his enthusiasm, energy and determined nature the Tiger will often rise to the top of his chosen profession.

In love, the Tiger is a romantic. He is sincere and open in his affections and has a passionate nature. He will devote himself entirely to the person of his affection and feelings will be intense. However, he does have a restless nature and in time his feelings may begin to wander.

The female Tiger has a warm and friendly nature. She is outgoing, sharp, ambitious and versatile. The Tigress takes an active interest in the education of her children and makes an admirable teacher.

At some time during his life the Tiger may be tempted to throw caution to the wind and go off and do what he wants to do: drop out of society for a time, travel the world or abandon his job to fulfil an ambition. The Tiger is a risk taker and a law unto himself.

Famous Tigers

Richard Branson, Tom Cruise, Marilyn Monroe, Demi Moore, The Queen, Oscar Wilde.

TIGER AND TIGER

General Relations

With his lively and outgoing nature the Tiger makes friends with ease. However, when it comes to his own sign relations are difficult. The Tiger is bold, forthright and likes to have his own way so when two Tigers come together they clash. Each tries to dominate the other and are both so independent-minded that neither really needs another strong-willed Tiger for companionship.

Working relations between two Tigers will again prove difficult. They are both competitive and, rather than pooling their resources and working as a team, they are more likely to end up competing against each other. They are too restless and too independent minded for any satisfactory working relationship to exist. As colleagues or business partners two Tigers will quickly go their own way.

In Love and Marriage

When two Tigers meet they may have much fun together, but the attraction between them could be short lived. This can be a difficult match.

Tigers like to retain a certain independence in their actions and this could put a strain on their relationship. Each wants to do his own thing in his own way and in time this desire for independence may become more pronounced. A Tiger couple can also be restless and there may be a distinct lack of stability in a Tiger household. Also, both tend to spend their money freely and together they may quickly deplete any savings.

Generally, although Tigers have many fine and admirable qualities, they are ill suited to each other. They are too dominant, too headstrong and too restless to live in harmony and it takes an exceptional Tiger couple to make this relationship work.

A difficult match

TIGER AND RABBIT

General Relations

The Tiger and Rabbit find each other interesting company. The Rabbit admires the Tiger's courage, zest and enthusiasm, while the Tiger values the Rabbit's discreet and companionable nature. Although they have very different personalities – the Tiger being far more outgoing and adventurous than the Rabbit – they respect each other and relations are reasonably good.

When the Tiger and Rabbit work together each benefits from the skills and strengths of the other. The Rabbit gains from the enthusiastic, enterprising and innovative nature of the Tiger, while the Tiger benefits from the planning and sound business sense of the Rabbit. The Rabbit also acts as a valuable restraining influence on some of the Tiger's more reckless notions. By combining their different skills they can make a fine team.

In Love and Marriage

There is considerable attraction between the Tiger and Rabbit. The Rabbit delights in the lively and vivacious nature of the Tiger, while the Tiger values the Rabbit's refined and sociable manner. Both are passionate and sensual signs and there is a strong physical attraction.

They are both keen socializers as well as creatures of comfort and enjoy leading an active social life. They benefit from each other's company; the Rabbit may become more assertive under the Tiger's influence, while the Tiger may become better organized and less impulsive. The Rabbit also acts as a steadying influence on the Tiger's restless nature.

However, to maintain their relationship each needs to show willingness to adjust to the other. The Rabbit needs to allow the Tiger independence rather than insist on complete togetherness, while the Tiger needs to be respectful of the Rabbit's feelings. Despite the differences between them, they appreciate each other's finer qualities and form a satisfying and fulfilling match.

An excellent match

TIGER AND DRAGON

General Relations

The Tiger and Dragon may enjoy each other's company for a time; both like to keep themselves active, enjoy socializing and travelling and may also share a fondness for outdoor activities. But in time their dominant and forceful personalities may clash, particularly as both can be so forthright when expressing their views and opinions.

In a working situation the Tiger and Dragon can make an effective combination. Both are enterprising and ambitious and between them they have a never-ending supply of ideas. They are also risk takers and can be bold and resourceful in their actions. Providing they do not over-reach themselves they can enjoy considerable success. They make a fine and dynamic duo.

In Love and Marriage

With their lively, passionate and outgoing natures, the Tiger and Dragon are often attracted to each other. In the early days of their relationship there is lots of passion, excitement and happiness. Both are keen socializers and travellers and both like to keep themselves occupied with a wide range of activites. Life in a Dragon-Tiger household is never dull!

However, both the Tiger and Dragon are forceful signs and like to have their own way. Both can be too forthright in their views and their frankness may lead to heated exchanges. They can also be restless and crave for a certain independence in their actions and this may put a strain on their relationship.

If the Tiger and Dragon are prepared to compromise they may be able to sustain the intensity of the early glorious days of their relationship.

An exciting – but challenging – match

TIGER AND SNAKE

General Relations

The Tiger and Snake do not relate well to each other. The Tiger is a strong-minded extrovert, while the Snake is an equally strong-minded introvert. The Snake is calm, orderly and reflective, while the Tiger is full of energy and verve. Apart from an occasional lively discussion, these two signs prefer to socialize with others more in tune with their own character.

When working together there may be a lack of trust between the Tiger and Snake. The Snake considers the Tiger reckless, while the Tiger is suspicious of the Snake's quiet and secretive nature. The Tiger is impulsive and action orientated while the Snake is more patient and calculating. If the two signs are prepared to go some way towards reconciling their differences, they may find each other benefiting from the other's strengths, but as both signs find it hard to like or trust the other, rarely does this happen.

In Love and Marriage

The Tiger and Snake are opposites and generally do not get on well. Although there may be some initial attraction between the two signs – the Tiger being enchanted by the seductive ways of the Snake and the Snake by the Tiger's lively nature – it is likely to be short-lived.

Tigers are action-orientated souls who like to live life to the full. The Snake, however, is calm, reflective and sets about life at his own pace. The Snake just cannot accept the bustle and vigour with which the Tiger chooses to conduct his activities, while the Tiger quickly loses patience with the slow and calculating ways of the Snake.

The Tiger also resents the possessiveness of a Snake partner. The Tiger likes to retain a degree of independence and the Snake views such an attitude with mistrust. As the Tiger tends to spend more freely than the Snake, there may be conflicts over money matters.

A difficult match

TIGER AND HORSE

General Relations

The Tiger and Horse are two lively and spirited individuals who get on well together. They share many interests, including a love of discussion, travel and the great outdoors and with their enthusiasm and energy they will have many good times together. They often become firm friends.

These two signs also work well together and, as colleagues or business partners, can enjoy considerable success. Both are bold, enterprising and work hard. Neither is afraid of taking risks and between them they are likely to devise many interesting projects. They trust and respect each other and while each can at times be volatile, the other sign often exercises a restraining influence. With their enthusiasm and determination, the Tiger and Horse make an awe-inspiring combination.

In Love and Marriage

The Tiger and Horse are both passionate and sensual signs and, with their good looks and lively personalities, they are often attracted to each other.

They share many interests, are keen socializers and possess adventurous spirits. However, what is particularly important in this match is that each recognizes that the other still needs a degree of independence. Both the Tiger and the Horse feel a necessity to have some freedom and appreciate the ability to go off and devote time to their own interests.

They both hold strong opinions and can be stubborn and headstrong, and while there may be times of disagreement, there is also a great deal of respect between the two signs and they are usually able to ride out any differences.

The Tiger and Horse also make dutiful and conscientious parents and although strict, they make sure their children want for nothing.

An excellent match

TIGER AND GOAT

General Relations

The Tiger and Goat get on well together and can become firm friends. The Goat admires the enterprise, vitality and confidence of the Tiger, while the Tiger enjoys the Goat's easygoing and sociable manner.

The Tiger and Goat can also work well together, particularly if their work is of a creative nature and allows each to generate ideas and make the most of their creative talents. The Tiger invariably takes the lead in any venture and is a valuable source of inspiration for the Goat. These two signs need, however, to deal with the financial aspects of any concern carefully as both tend to be free in their spending.

In Love and Marriage

There is considerable attraction between the Tiger and Goat and, in love and marriage, they can find happiness. The Tiger is passionate, the Goat amorous and the physical attraction between them is strong.

The Goat enjoys the lively and enterprising nature of the Tiger, and the Goat values his sincere and honourable ways. The Tiger, too, delights in the Goat's genial and sociable nature, and he finds the Goat affectionate, caring and extremely supportive.

Both signs are great socializers, and between them have a wide circle of friends. Both also have creative and imaginative natures. However, in order to maintain their love they need to show some willingness to adapt. The Tiger – who can be forthright in his views – may upset the more sensitive Goat. The Goat, in turn needs to allow the Tiger time to pursue his own interests. Both signs tend to be carefree spenders.

Provided they are prepared to adapt to each other they can look forward to a contented life together.

A good match

TIGER AND MONKEY

General Relations

The Tiger and Monkey are two lively, forceful and outgoing signs. Although they can get on well together, each is still slightly wary of the other. The honourable Tiger is distrustful of the Monkey's sometimes cunning and devious nature, while the Monkey resists the Tiger's domineering attitude. In terms of casual friendship and for socializing, these two signs can enjoy each other's company, but problems could emerge if their friendship goes any deeper.

When the Tiger and Monkey work together their different personalities may cause problems. Although they are both ambitious and enterprising, the Tiger cannot abide some of the Monkey's more devious notions, while the Monkey does not tolerate the Tiger's authoritarian stance. Unless united by a particular goal, they are likely to drift apart.

In Love and Marriage

When the Tiger and Monkey first fall in love, there is passion, excitement and lots of optimism for the future. However, their hopes may soon turn sour and, unless both are prepared to adapt, the long-term prospects may be difficult.

Both signs are forceful, determined and like to have things their own way. The Tiger is honest and open in his feelings, while the Monkey can sometimes be evasive; such an attitude may prove intensely irritating to the Tiger. The Monkey, who likes to keep tabs on everything, is suspicious of the Tiger's desire for freedom in his actions and the Tiger may come to resent the Monkey's inquisitive and sometimes interfering nature. In times of disagreement both signs can be notoriously stubborn. Both can also be very competitive and this 'power struggle' for dominance, together with a mistrust of each other's motives, may undermine their relationship.

A difficult match

TIGER AND ROOSTER

General Relations

The Tiger and Rooster have several traits in common; both like socializing and have lively and outgoing natures. But they both can be forceful and each may want to dominate the other. They can also be candid and forthright, and when such frankness overflows any accord that existed quickly degenerates.

In business each sign may gain much from the other. The Tiger benefits from the Rooster's more methodical and consistent manner, while the Rooster gains from the Tiger's innovative ideas and enterprise. Their individual strengths may complement each other, but first they need to settle their differences. Both can be competitive and each wants to take the lead. If both signs are prepared to pool their strengths for a common objective, then they may make an effective partnership. But, more times than not, their conflicting natures come to the fore and undermine their efforts.

In Love and Marriage

Initially there may be a strong attraction between the Tiger and Rooster, both physical and mental. Each admires the strength and confidence of the other and both are keen socializers. However, the longer-term prospects for their relationship may prove difficult.

The Rooster is a great organizer and, to the less disciplined Tiger, he may at times appear fussy and pedantic. Should the Tiger vent these feelings, strong words will be exchanged as the Rooster does not take criticism lightly.

Similarly, the Tiger's impulsive nature disturbs the Rooster's sense of routine. The Rooster likes to keep tabs on everything around him and this is just not possible with a Tiger about.

Basically, due to their frank, determined and stubborn natures, a match between a Tiger and Rooster is far from easy. To succeed they must accept the other for what they are, recognize their different personalities and allow each other enough freedom to pursue their individual interests.

A difficult match

TIGER AND DOG

General Relations

The Tiger and Dog get on well together and can become firm friends. There is much trust and understanding between them and each benefits from the other's strengths. The Dog admires the enthusiasm and courage of the Tiger but is a steadying influence on his restless nature. The Tiger in turn values the Dog's loyal and dependable nature and does much to dispel the Dog's worrying and pessimistic tendencies.

The Tiger and Dog also work well together. They trust and respect each other and can form a successful team. The Dog feels inspired and motivated by the enthusiasm of the Tiger, while the Tiger is mindful of the Dog's often cautionary but wise advice. The Tiger and Dog are loyal to each other and by combining their different skills and qualities they can enjoy considerable success.

In Love and Marriage

Although there are personality differences between the Tiger and Dog, they complement each other extremely well.

Both the Tiger and the Dog are loyal, trusting and honourable and each values these qualities in the other. There is an excellent rapport and understanding between them. The pessimistic Dog can find reassurance and support from the more confident Tiger. The Dog, too, admires the courage, willpower and altruism of the Tiger. The Tiger inspires the Dog and the Dog in turn is loyal, supportive and loving.

Each does much to help the other and as a couple they quickly become devoted to each other. They also both possess a caring and humanitarian nature and may be united in helping those less fortunate than themselves.

If the two signs have a family they make admirable parents and, with the Tiger's adventurous spirit and the Dog's caring nature, they are a delight for any children.

An excellent match

TIGER AND PIG

General Relations

Lively, sociable and with many interests in common, the Tiger and Pig get on well together. The Tiger enjoys the Pig's good-natured company as well as valuing the Pig's sincerity and integrity. Similarly, the Pig delights in the Tiger's honest and open manner as well as appreciating his energy and enterprising nature. These two signs understand each other well and can become firm friends.

The Tiger and Pig are better suited on a social rather than business level, but when they work together they can still benefit from each other's strengths. Both are ambitious and both work hard but the Tiger's impulsive, impatient and generous nature may be of concern to the more patient and financially astute Pig. However, if committed to a specific objective their combined strengths can often lead them to success.

In Love and Marriage

The Tiger and Pig are often attracted to each other and make a splendid match. Both are passionate and sensual signs and there is a strong physical attraction.

Together they have many interests they can share. Both are keen socializers, take pleasure in entertaining and devote much energy to their home and family. The Pig, who understands the Tiger so well, does not begrudge the Tiger the liberty he needs.

The patient Pig is a stabilizing influence on the restless Tiger and is a useful curb on some of the Tiger's more impulsive notions. The Tiger benefits from the Pig's wise counsel and financial judgement. The Tiger, in turn, is of great help to the Pig. The Pig feels inspired and motivated by the enthusiasm of the Tiger and the Tiger encourages him to realize his true potential. Also the Pig, with his deep faith in human nature, can sometimes be naive and vulnerable and the Tiger provides protection and support.

A splendid couple

THE RABBIT

Key characteristics:

Sociable, discreet, refined, shrewd, perceptive,
sensitive, aloof.

In love:

Romantic, passionate and a good judge of character.

The fourth Chinese sign is governed by virtue and prudence
and has a refined and sociable manner. He prefers the
quieter things in life and sets about his activities in an
unflustered way. He enjoys conversation and he often dis-
penses wise and shrewd advice.

The Rabbit usually has a happy and contented disposition. He dislikes arguments and will do his utmost to avoid
any sort of unpleasantness. He feels life is to be savoured

and he sometimes shuts himself off from some of the harsher aspects.

The female Rabbit carries herself with much dignity and is often an elegant woman. She is softly spoken and has an affectionate nature. She frequently has a circle of close friends and is greatly admired for her discretion and understanding.

The male Rabbit is also popular. Often good looking, he has considerable charm and his agreeable manner will win him many friends.

The Rabbit has a romantic and passionate nature and is likely to have many romances before settling down. He is a good judge of character and usually makes a fine choice of partner. Although they tend to have large families, the responsibilities of parenthood do not always come easily. Some Rabbits find children a disruptive influence on their otherwise orderly lifestyle and have difficulty in coping with their more boisterous antics.

Famous Rabbits

Ingrid Bergman, Cary Grant, George Michael, Roger Moore, Frank Sinatra, Queen Victoria.

RABBIT AND RABBIT

General Relations

The Rabbit is one of the most companionable signs in the Chinese zodiac and two Rabbits can get on extremely well together. They have similar interests, particularly a love of conversation, and an appreciation of the finer things in life. There is trust and understanding between them and a noticeable absence of discord. They enjoy each other's company and can become firm friends.

Rabbits are careful and shrewd workers and when they work together, either as colleagues or business partners. They both possess fine judgement, good financial skills and commercial acumen and there is a good level of trust and understanding between them. Neither is given to taking risks and through careful planning and determination, two Rabbits can do well. Their enterprise may not be the most dynamic, but it is certainly founded on solid principles.

In Love and Marriage

With their romantic and passionate natures Rabbits are often attracted to each other. They share similar interests and outlooks and there is a close affinity between them. Both strive to establish a stable, secure and harmonious relationship and go to great lengths to avoid arguments.

The two Rabbits enjoy conversation, have an interest in the arts and the countryside and are keen socializers. They also both devote much time, energy and expense in creating and maintaining their home. Rabbits place much importance on their house and often stay in the same place for a long time.

A Rabbit couple do much to support each other. Both are conscientious and careful workers, have good financial judgement and take much pleasure in entertaining.

A loving couple

RABBIT AND DRAGON

General Relations

The Rabbit and Dragon can get on reasonably well together and, while their interests may not always coincide, they respect and like each other. The Rabbit appreciates the openness, sincerity and integrity of the Dragon, while the Dragon values the finesse and quiet, discreet manner of the Rabbit. Although the Dragon may enjoy a more energetic lifestyle to the Rabbit, these two signs can become trusted friends and confidantes.

The Rabbit and Dragon also work well together and their collective talents can make a successful combination. The Dragon's enthusiasm and drive will be of great benefit to the more cautious Rabbit, while the Rabbit's diplomacy, commercial acumen and more methodical nature helps the Dragon. Provided each is aware of their individual roles and remain committed to a specific objective, they can make a good and productive team.

In Love and Marriage

With both signs being passionate and alluring, the Rabbit and Dragon are certainly attracted to each other and the early stages of their romance are truly blissful. However, if they are to sustain the deep love they feel for each other, both need to reconcile their different personalities.

The Dragon is far more outgoing than the Rabbit and likes to lead an active life, while the Rabbit is more restrained and prefers the quieter things in life. If both signs accept that they do have different interests and allow each other personal freedom they can find great contentment.

They can also gain from their different qualities. The Dragon, who can be blunt and forthright, learns much from the more gracious and tactful Rabbit, while the Rabbit benefits from the Dragon's confident and outgoing nature. They are also both astute and diligent workers and between them have considerable earning ability.

A good match

RABBIT AND SNAKE

General Relations

The Rabbit and Snake have much in common and can get on well together. Both are quiet, thoughtful signs; they are good natured and have a liking for the finer things in life. They share many interests and, with their love of conversation, pass many a happy hour in deep and wide-ranging discussion. They respect and understand each other and can become firm friends. General relations between these two signs are invariably good.

There is also the potential for the Rabbit and Snake to form a good working relationship. Both are skilled in financial matters and have considerable commercial acumen. Between them they have ideas and skills but tend to be cautious and great deliberators. However when they are firing on all cylinders they make a formidable and successful team.

In Love and Marriage

The Rabbit and Snake are often deeply attracted to each other and in love and marriage they can find much happiness. Both are gentle, reflective signs who thrive in an orderly, secure and stable environment.

Both may have a liking for the arts and literature and share an appreciation of the finer things in life. They take great delight in furnishing their home to make it extremely comfortable. Both Rabbits and Snakes are creatures of comfort and they enjoy many a pleasant evening sitting in their perfectly created lair relaxing.

Both Rabbit and Snake are perceptive and intuitive (even psychically gifted) signs and do much to help and assist the other. The one difficulty that may arise stems from the Snake's possessiveness – he demands great loyalty. The Rabbit may wish to pursue some independent interests and, for both their sakes, the Snake must allow this.

A successful match

RABBIT AND HORSE

General Relations

The Rabbit and Horse have very different temperaments and this does not make for good relations. The Horse has an active and outgoing nature and likes to live life to the full. The Rabbit, however, is much calmer and more placid and feels ill at ease with the energetic, lively and assertive Horse. Admittedly both are eloquent and persuasive speakers and may enjoy time together in conversation, but generally there is a certain coolness and reserve between them and they rarely become close friends.

This lack of rapport is also evident when they work together. The Horse is enterprising, while the Rabbit is cautious. The Rabbit considers the Horse rash and impulsive, while the Horse views the Rabbit as a restraining influence. Differences over finance could emerge; the Horse spends freely and is a great risk-taker. Unless committed to a specific objective, they do not work well together.

In Love and Marriage

Although relations between the Rabbit and Horse may not always be the best, these two signs can still fall very much in love. For all their differences, they each possess qualities that the other admires. They both have a strong sense of integrity, are discreet and trusting and both have a fondness for conversation and dialogue. There is also a strong physical attraction.

However, while the early stages of their romance promise so much, the love and affection they feel for each other may be difficult to sustain. The Rabbit seeks a secure, tranquil and orderly existence and may feel unsettled by the Horse's restless and volatile nature. The Horse also has a temper which, although often short lived, again unnerves the Rabbit. The Horse, however, may feel resentful that the Rabbit is not as willing to share in his many activities as he would like. The Rabbit is much more of a homelover than the Horse. In addition, their different attitudes towards money may pose problems.

A turbulent match

RABBIT AND GOAT

General Relations

The Rabbit and Goat get on very well together and can become firm friends. They share many interests and both have a liking for the finer things in life. They relate well to each other and as both possess quiet and placid natures, each feels secure and contented in the company of the other.

The trust that exists between the Rabbit and the Goat also helps them when they work together. To do well the Goat often needs a motivating force behind him and the Rabbit provides this. Calm, methodical and financially astute, the Rabbit is an inspiration for the Goat and as a result the Goat gives his best, providing support, creativity and innovation.

In Love and Marriage

The attraction between the Rabbit and Goat is strong and in love and marriage they can be blissfully happy. They are well suited and their many mutual interests and similar outlooks make them highly compatible. Both are genial, peaceloving signs who strive to make their lives secure and stable. They both appreciate the finer things in life and work to maintain a high standard of living.

There is a good understanding and rapport between the Rabbit and Goat and they offer each other much love, affection and loyalty. The main danger to their relationship is if some calamity should strike. Neither copes well under stress and a crisis may easily undermine the harmonious existence they have built up. However, as far as possible, these two signs do their utmost to avoid anything which would jeopardize their comfortable existence and more often than not go through life savouring the fruits of their labours and loving and supporting each other.

An excellent match

RABBIT AND MONKEY

General Relations

For all their many differences, the Rabbit and Monkey get on well and can become good friends. The Monkey is quick to appreciate the Rabbit's good sense, quiet confidence and companionable nature, while the Rabbit enjoys the Monkey's zest, sparkle and resourcefulness. Both have wide interests, keen intellects and a love of conversation. They may spend many enjoyable times in each other's company.

When the Rabbit and Monkey work together relations between them may not be so favourable. The Rabbit is honest and ethical in his business dealings and is greatly concerned by the Monkey's sometimes dubious and crafty ploys. Nor is the Rabbit prepared to share in the risks that the enterprising Monkey wants to take and the Monkey may find the Rabbit a restraining and inhibiting influence.

In Love and Marriage

While the Rabbit and Monkey may have very distinct personalities, these two signs complement each other well. In love and marriage they can make a loyal, happy and contented pair.

The Monkey is the more outgoing of the two signs and the Rabbit delights in the Monkey's wit, confidence and self-assured nature. Admittedly the Rabbit may not like some of the uncertainty and unpredictability that goes with a highly spirited Monkey, or, indeed, some of the Monkey's more crafty notions, but the Rabbit does value and appreciate the Monkey's skills. Similarly, the Monkey regards the Rabbit as a wise, loving and loyal partner. The Rabbit provides stability and order and the Monkey appreciates this.

The one factor which could disturb their relationship is the Rabbit's inability to cope with the Monkey's restlessness. However, both signs mean much to each other and both do much to overcome any difficulties.

A good match

RABBIT AND ROOSTER

General Relations

Relations between these two signs are poor. Their different personalities just do not gel and neither feels at ease in the company of the other. The Rooster is much too forthright and candid for the Rabbit's liking – the Rabbit can be sensitive and loathes criticism – while the Rooster finds the Rabbit reserved and withdrawn.

When the Rabbit and Rooster are colleagues or business partners again relations may prove difficult. Although both are methodical, work hard and are honourable in their dealings, their different personalities bring them into conflict. The Rabbit just does not tolerate the bossiness, fussiness or domineering attitude of the Rooster, while the Rooster does not care much for the Rabbit's quiet, patient and more cautious manner. The Rooster likes hustle and bustle and activity and that is just not the way of the Rabbit.

In Love and Marriage

This is a challenging match – the introverted Rabbit and the extroverted Rooster. Although each may recognize the other's qualities, their different personalities may present them with many difficulties.

The Rabbit is quiet, refined and tactful, while the Rooster can be brash, flamboyant and candid. Many times the sensitive Rabbit is unnerved or feels uncomfortable at the Rooster's utterances. If a Rabbit-Rooster relationship stands any chance of surviving, the Rooster needs to be much more diplomatic and more aware of the Rabbit's feelings.

The Rabbit also craves a quiet and peaceful existence, while the Rooster likes to lead a more active and energetic lifestyle. In view of their different personalities it takes an exceptional couple to make this relationship work.

A difficult match

RABBIT AND DOG

General Relations

Rabbits and Dogs like each other and relations between them are good. They are both loyal and caring signs and often share similar interests and outlooks. There is much respect and understanding between them and they relate well to each other.

On a business level, they are both diligent and hard working. When things are going well the Rabbit and Dog make a powerful team – it is only when they face problems or a downturn in activity that the difficulties emerge. The Dog is prone to bouts of anxiety and the Rabbit does not cope well under stress; difficult situations may put serious strains on an otherwise excellent working relationship.

In Love and Marriage

The Rabbit and Dog have much in common and are often deeply attracted to each other. Both seek a stable and secure existence and there is a good level of trust between them. In love and marriage the Rabbit and Dog are well suited.

Both attach much importance to their home and, with the Rabbit's fine artistic taste and the Dog's practical skills, their home is a pride to both. The two signs also take much pleasure in entertaining their friends.

They also appreciate each other's qualities. The Rabbit delights in the loyalty, dependability and sincerity of the Dog, while the Dog values the refined and companionable ways of the Rabbit. They also do much to help each other. Both are prone to periods of self-doubt. The Dog tends to be a worrier, while the Rabbit does not cope well under stress. Each is a useful prop for the other and together they give each other valuable support.

An excellent couple

RABBIT AND PIG

General Relations

Both Rabbits and Pigs are highly sociable signs and can get on well together. They often share similar interests and there is a good rapport between them. They respect and understand each other well and, while the Pig may not always be as refined as the Rabbit may wish, general relations between these two signs are invariably good.

The Chinese consider that Pigs are lucky in business and money matters and this, combined with the Rabbit's shrewd sense, makes a working relationship between these two signs highly favourable. Both work hard and their persistence and determination helps them in any venture. Each also gains from the other. The Rabbit feels reassured by having such an honourable, robust and resilient partner, while the Pig values the Rabbit's organizational abilities and perceptive advice.

In Love and Marriage

The Rabbit and Pig are highly compatible and in love and marriage they can find much happiness. They share many interests – particularly a love of the countryside and nature – and enjoy an active social life. They are also both peaceloving signs and go to great lengths to avoid arguments and disputes.

Both are also passionate and sensual signs and there is a strong physical attraction between them.

The Rabbit and Pig are also respectful of each other's feelings. The Pig is far more resilient than the Rabbit and the Pig makes every effort to shoulder many of the burdens that can so vex the Rabbit. Similarly, the Rabbit acts as a trusted adviser for the Pig, giving advice that the Pig, sometimes gullible and naive, greatly benefits from.

An ideal match

THE DRAGON

Key characteristics:

Active, determined, confident, enterprising, versatile,
scrupulous and lucky.

In love:

Passionate, faithful and sincere but demanding!

Flamboyant, colourful and vibrant, the dragon makes a
splendid leader of the carnival. Governed by luck, this sign
has a lively and outgoing nature, a quick mind and is pos-
sessed with much energy and enthusiasm. He is a doer and
an achiever, and has a most determined nature. With his
confident and self-assured manner he has considerable
leadership qualities. The Dragon thrives on challenges and
is constantly setting himself new goals.

Exuberant and confident, the Dragon tends to be at the forefront of whatever he is doing. To some extent he is a showman and he likes to be noticed and win the approval of others. Similarly, in matters of the heart he will never be short of admirers. He has style, grace and allure and with his lively and sociable nature makes fascinating company.

If he has children the Dragon can be a firm but loving parent. He will be quick to spot where his children's talents lie and will do much to encourage and support them. However, he does have high expectations for them and sets high standards. He also expects to be obeyed and woe betide any children who flout his authority.

The female Dragon is versatile and highly gifted. She is popular, will have many friends and carries herself with considerable aplomb. The male Dragon is self-assured in his manner and keen to make the most of his abilities.

Famous Dragons

Jeffrey Archer, Julie Christie, Salvador Dali, Matt Dillon, John Lennon, Abraham Lincoln, Al Pacino.

DRAGON AND DRAGON

General Relations

Dragons are lively and sociable signs and for a time two Dragons can get on well together. They enjoy each other's company and have a lively exchange of views. However, Dragons can also be domineering and forthright and, in time, their interests may clash. For the short to medium term general relations between two Dragons are good; after that difficulties may emerge.

Dragons are enterprising and diligent workers and when two Dragons work together, they can make a formidable team. They both set high standards and are enthusiastic, determined and ambitious. When they are committed to a particular objective, their combined strengths – together with their luck – help them to success. However, both are assertive and domineering characters and they would do well to agree upon a division of responsibilities. If not, they may end up vying with each other for control and thereby undermining a successful working partnership.

In Love and Marriage

Dragons are often attracted to each other. When in love they can be passionately happy – they have fun and excitement and together will talk of great plans, of hopes and of the opportunities that await them. Their love and devotion to each other is total.

However, they need to proceed carefully if they are to maintain such a happy and harmonious state. Both can be stubborn and forthright and, with their forceful and domineering natures, each strives to get their own way. It is also in their interests if they have a clear division of responsibilities and try not to interfere too much in each other's duties.

If they can come to terms with their dominant and strong-willed natures two Dragons can make a dynamic, outgoing and striking couple and their life together is rich and fulfilling.

An ideal match

DRAGON AND SNAKE

General Relations

Relations between the Dragon and Snake are excellent. They understand and trust each other and there is great respect between them. The Dragon values the Snake's wisdom and perceptiveness, while the Snake is intoxicated by the charm, zest and dynamism of the Dragon. The Dragon and Snake genuinely like and admire each other and can become lifelong friends.

A business relationship between these two signs can also be successful, with each sign benefiting from the strengths and skills of the other. The Snake is shrewd, calculating and plans his activities with the utmost care and is a useful check on some of the Dragon's more rash and impulsive notions. Similarly, the vigour and enthusiasm with which the Dragon conducts his activities is an important stimulus for the Snake. In business, they can enjoy great success.

In Love and Marriage

The Dragon and Snake make an excellent match and in love and marriage can find much happiness.

There is a strong attraction between these signs, both physical and mental. The calm, alluring and seductive charms of the Snake prove irresistible to the Dragon, while the Snake is attracted by the warmth, vitality and sincerity of the Dragon. Each will benefit from the qualities of the other and there is a great deal of trust and understanding between them.

The one problem that may emerge in this relationship stems from the Snake's possessiveness. If the Dragon should ever give the Snake grounds for jealously, or finds the Snake's possessiveness too great, difficulties may arise. But generally such a problem is a rare occurrence.

An ideal match

DRAGON AND HORSE

General Relations

There is a liking and respect between these two signs and for a time general relations are good. Both are lively and adventurous characters and there is trust and understanding between them. For the short to medium term they can become almost inseparable friends, but each sign possesses an independent streak and, unless there is a romantic involvement, over time they may well decide to go their separate ways.

Both are diligent and hard workers and, when committed to a specific goal, their enthusiasm leads them to considerable success. They also benefit from each other's strengths. The Dragon possesses a stronger imagination and vision than the Horse, while the Horse is more practical and realistic. By combining their skills they create a powerful force. However, both signs are ambitious and strong willed and in time new challenges, together with a desire to prove themselves on their own, may eventually pull them apart.

In Love and Marriage

There is considerable attraction between the Dragon and Horse. Both are lively and outgoing signs. Both are attractive and presentable and, with their good looks and engaging personalities, each is drawn to the other. They are both passionate and amorous signs and the early stages of their romance are blissful.

Both are forceful and domineering signs and, unless they can agree on a clear division of responsibilities in their home life, there may be tussles between them. Both can be forthright in expressing their views and, with the Horse's temper and the Dragon's frankness, life at times may become heated. Horses can also be self-centred and Dragons demanding, so sometimes their personalities and viewpoints clash. All these areas may undermine their relationship but with goodwill and understanding they should be able to reconcile any differences that may occur.

A good match

DRAGON AND GOAT

General Relations

The Dragon and Goat get on reasonably well together. The Goat delights in the Dragon's lively and confident manner, while the Dragon admires the Goat's sociable and creative nature. However, in time, the Dragon may begin to lose patience with the Goat's capricious and fickle ways and the Goat, always keen to make new friends, may forsake the Dragon for other company; rarely is this a long-lasting friendship.

A Dragon and Goat can, for a time, work reasonably well together. The Dragon, who is far more assertive than the Goat, takes the lead in any enterprise and is a valuable source of motivation for the Goat. When united in pursuing a specific objective they can make a successful combination although, with the Dragon's restlessness and Goat's capriciousness, the durability of their working relationship may not be great.

In Love and Marriage

The attraction between the Dragon and Goat can be great and these two signs can fall very much in love. Both signs are highly sociable and have lively temperaments. There is also a strong physical attraction between them and their sex life is immensely satisfying for both.

The Dragon feels heartened by the Goat's devotion and reliance and the Goat is comforted and reassured by the Dragon. A romance between them is something neither ever forgets. Unfortunately this happy state of affairs may not continue in marriage.

The Goat can be temperamental and capricious and the Dragon may quickly tire of his fickle nature and mood swings. Similarly, the Goat feels ill at ease with the Dragon's restless and independent nature. For a marriage to succeed, there needs to be much understanding on both sides and this may prove difficult.

A challenging match

DRAGON AND MONKEY

General Relations

The Dragon and Monkey are two lively and sociable signs and they get on well together. They both enjoy each other's company and, with their many mutual interests and energetic natures, they can become lifelong friends. There is trust and understanding between them and should either suffer a reversal in fortune – as, indeed, could be likely, as both are risk takers – the other is there to support and advise.

This rapport also assists them when they work together. Both signs are resourceful and set about their activities with enthusiasm. The Monkey is adept at spotting opportunities and the Dragon is certainly not averse to taking risks. Admittedly their impetuous natures may sometimes lead them into difficulties, but the Monkey is an expert at extricating himself and others from problems and their skills, enterprise and sheer ability win them through.

In Love and Marriage

The Dragon and Monkey are ideally suited to each other and in love and marriage they can establish a tender, caring and loving relationship. Both signs are lively and outgoing and possess energy and enthusiasm.

The Dragon greatly admires the Monkey for his wit, guile and talent. Similarly, the Monkey values the Dragon's bold and confident manner. The Dragon is sincere and trusting and, like the Monkey, is prepared to stand up for what he believes and go after what he wants. Both are action orientated and as a couple they work as a team, each helping the other with his various activities.

Both the Dragon and Monkey can be flamboyant in their gestures and, to some, they might appear an eccentric or unconventional couple, but neither cares, as their feelings for each other are so strong.

A good match

DRAGON AND ROOSTER

General Relations

The Dragon and Rooster have much in common. They are lively and spirited signs, both with a mind of their own. They are keen socializers, share many interests and enjoy each other's company. Both like to make full use of their time and both are outgoing and enterprising. General relations between them are invariably good.

The Dragon and Rooster can also form a useful working relationship. The Rooster gains from the vision and enthusiasm of the Dragon, while the Dragon benefits from the organizational skills of the Rooster. The Rooster is also a useful curb on some of the Dragon's more reckless notions. They are both diligent and hard workers.

In Love and Marriage

The Dragon and Rooster make a good match and in love and marriage they find happiness together.

The more conservative Rooster is a stabilizing influence on the Dragon and provides order and planning to the Dragon's hectic lifestyle. Similarly the Dragon helps to break down some of the Rooster's reserve. They also allow each other time to maintain their own separate interests; something which is essential for both.

The main problem in their relationship is that both can be notoriously forthright in expressing their views. The Rooster is famed for being candid and the Dragon is certainly no diplomat; as a result they are likely to have many heated discussions.

With some of the other Chinese signs, the Dragon outshines and dominates his partner, but not so with the Rooster. Each plays an equal part in their relationship and together they weather the storms, helping each other all the way.

A good match

DRAGON AND DOG

General Relations

There is little accord between the Dragon and Dog and general relations between these two signs are poor. Their outlooks and personalities are often very different and neither has much time for the other. The Dog sees the Dragon as being brash and opinionated, while the Dragon has little patience for the serious and sometimes moralizing tones of the Dog. These signs rarely become friends.

Their lack of rapport also hampers business relationships. Both find it hard to trust the other and there may well be a battle for supremacy. The Dog is critical of the Dragon's enterprising and sometimes risky notions, while the Dragon finds the Dog's cautionary approach too much of a restrictive influence.

In Love and Marriage

Tradition does not bode well for relations between the Dragon and Dog and, in love and marriage, there may be difficulties.

The essential problem lies in their different personalities. The Dragon is lively and outgoing, while the Dog is a direct, matter-of-fact and no-nonsense sort of person. The Dragon's showiness does not wash with the Dog, and the Dog also finds it hard to trust or relate to such an impulsive and impetuous character. Similarly, the Dragon finds it hard to understand the personality of the Dog.

The two signs tend to have different interests. The Dog is often very involved in humanitarian matters and much prefers a quiet meal with friends to partying. The Dragon, on the other hand, likes to be very much at the centre of things and enjoys an active social life.

A difficult match

DRAGON AND PIG

General Relations

The Dragon and Pig enjoy each other's company and general relations between them are good. Both are lively and sociable signs and they like to live life to the full. They both enjoy an active social life and are respectful of each other's views.

The Dragon and Pig work well together and can form a successful working relationship. The Dragon is born under the sign of luck and the Pig is generally fortunate in financial matters; together they can do well. They trust each other and both attach much importance to honesty and openness in their business dealings. The Pig benefits from the Dragon's enterprise and enthusiasm, while the Dragon gains from the Pig's more persistent and patient manner. Both are hard working and keen to give of their best.

In Love and Marriage

There is a considerable attraction between these two signs and in love and marriage the Dragon and Pig can form a close and loving relationship.

The Dragon is very much taken with the Pig's jovial company and admires his trusting and honourable nature. The Pig is a most attentive and caring partner and this is something that the Dragon readily appreciates. The Pig also gains much from a Dragon partner; the Dragon is a shield for the gullible Pig.

Both are hard-working signs and between them have considerable earning abilities. Many Dragon-Pig couples are materially well off and are able to put much energy into creating and maintaining their home.

A well-suited couple

THE SNAKE

Key characteristics:

Thoughtful, wise, shrewd, intuitive, guarded, independent, sometimes lazy.

In love:

Passionate, seductive and possessive!

The Snake is governed by wisdom and has a sharp and penetrating mind. With a quiet and reserved temperament, he chooses his friends with care and does not willingly let others into his confidence. He can be secretive and in many matters chooses to be his own master. Some may find his manner cool and evasive but should they try to penetrate through his reserve they will discover a warm and gentle character.

The Snake is best suited to more cerebral occupations

and often succeeds in careers such as teaching, politics, writing, science and the law. He does not enjoy manual labour. Ideally the Snake prefers to take his time in conducting his various activities.

The female Snake has style and grace. She chooses her clothes carefully and often adorns herself with beautiful jewellery. The male Snake, too, prides himself on his appearance and carries himself with considerable dignity.

With his wide interests, quiet manner and good humour, the Snake exudes charm. He is romantic, seductive and passionate – almost the Don Juan of the Chinese signs – and he does not lack admirers. For some his possessiveness may become too overbearing, but many enjoy the love, affection and security that the Snake gives.

The Snake has a complex personality. Wise, alert, and refined, the Snake is his own man. But behind this there lurks gentleness, good humour and powerful sensuality. The Snake has much to offer and throughout his life he will endeavour to give of his best and make the most of his considerable abilities.

Famous Snakes

Muhammad Ali, Kim Basinger, Tony Blair, Pierce Brosnan, Greta Garbo, John. F. Kennedy, Pablo Picasso.

SNAKE AND SNAKE

General Relations

On a purely social level the Snake enjoys the company of another Snake. Being such deep thinkers they delight in exchanging their views and their discussions are often profound and intellectually stimulating. Snakes find each other challenging company and general relations between them can, for a time, be good.

When two Snakes work together their relations are amiable and they may enjoy some measure of success, but generally this is not the best of combinations. Snakes are thoughtful creatures, given to periods of deliberation and reflection. Together they may create some wonderful and original ideas, but there may be long delays before they put their plans into action. To fulfil his potential the Snake really needs a partner who is more dynamic and action-orientated than another meditative and cautious Snake.

In Love and Marriage

Snakes can bewitch and mesmerize each other. With their strong seductive powers and their many mutual interests, Snakes can easily fall for one another and a love affair will be intense and sexually very active.

A Snake couple strives for a quiet and orderly existence. Both are artistically inclined and enjoy literature, music and the arts. They have enquiring minds and enjoy conversing about all manner of subjects. However, there are problems that they need to address.

The Snake is a possessive creature and each Snake keeps close tabs on the other. If either gives the other any cause for jealousy, there may be great problems between them. Also, as Snakes are so exclusive, there is a danger that a Snake couple may keep themselves to themselves to such a degree they may become stale and bored.

In love and marriage, from an intense start, the long-term prospects may prove challenging.

A difficult match

SNAKE AND HORSE

General Relations

The Snake and Horse find each other interesting company and relations between them are cordial, although not necessarily close. The Horse recognizes the Snake's sharp and incisive mind and values the Snake's opinions, while the Snake delights in the Horse's charming and eloquent manner. However, the Horse has an adventurous and independent spirit and relations may cool as the Snake dislikes the Horse's more active lifestyle.

As business partners the Snake and Horse make a reasonably good combination. The Snake thinks and plans, while the Horse put the plans into action. The hard-working Horse motivates the Snake and helps the Snake to become more action-orientated. The Snake, in turn, provides the Horse with much useful advice and also prevents the Horse from acting rashly.

In Love and Marriage

The attraction between the Snake and Horse can be strong and their relations intense. The Horse falls for the seductive charms of the Snake, while the Snake delights in the passion of the Horse.

There are problems in the long-term as they have very different personalities; however if the two signs develop an understanding of the other these differences can be overcome. The Snake can be possessive and the Horse may feel restricted by the Snake's attitude. The Snake, who can be promiscuous, also needs to curb his flirtatious nature. The Horse is faithful and loyal and expects the same from his partner.

The Horse is much more lively and adventurous than the Snake and he needs to recognize that the Snake cannot be hurried against his will; the Horse needs to develop a great deal of patience.

With care and understanding both can gain from their relationship, but for the match to survive they must each adapt to the other.

A challenging match

SNAKE AND GOAT

General Relations

The Snake and Goat are both calm and easygoing signs and general relations between them are good. With their mutual appreciation of the arts and their imaginative natures they have many interests in common. They are both connoisseurs of good food and drink and they pass many a happy hour in each other's company.

The Snake and Goat also work well together and, if their work is of a creative nature, they may enjoy much success. In their work the Goat benefits from the Snake's wise counsel and quiet determination, while the Snake gains from the Goat's inventive and original mind. There is a good rapport between them, although they need to exercise care when dealing with finance. Both signs can be indulgent and may find their spending quickly depletes any profits they make.

In Love and Marriage

The Snake and Goat are often attracted to each other and in love and marriage they can find much happiness. Both signs have a quiet and easygoing disposition and feel comfortable in each other's company. They share many interests, particularly of an artistic nature, and together they may enjoy music, literature, the theatre or some other aspect of the arts. The one problem that could beset them is that both can be indulgent and, despite the Snake's financial acumen, their money and savings may be quickly spent.

Although the Snake may at times despair over the Goat's capricious nature, they do support and encourage each other in their various endeavours. The Goat draws strength from the Snake's quiet and determined manner, while the Snake appreciates the originality and artistic talents of the Goat.

A well suited couple

SNAKE AND MONKEY

General Relations

On a social level the Snake and Monkey can get on reasonably well. Although they have different temperaments – the Snake being quiet and placid and the Monkey more lively and outgoing – there is considerable respect and liking between them. The Snake enjoys the Monkey's sparkling company and is enchanted by the Monkey's lively and resourceful nature, while the Monkey values the Snake's calm and thoughtful ways.

However, when the Snake and Monkey work together relations between them may prove difficult. The Snake is thoughtful, cautious and calculating, while the Monkey is geared up for action. The Monkey may view the Snake as a restraining influence, while the Snake considers the Monkey over-hasty and too impulsive. Both can be evasive and secretive and they are likely to keep their ideas and plans to themselves.

In Love and Marriage

The Snake and Monkey are two of the most complex signs in the Chinese zodiac; the Snake because he keeps his thoughts and emotions so close to his chest, while the Monkey is an expert at concealing his feelings behind his genial and personable nature. It is perhaps because of their complexity that the Snake and Monkey intrigue each other and are drawn together. Once entwined, they rarely separate.

In a Snake-Monkey match each benefits from the qualities and skills of the other. The Snake delights in the Monkey's ebullient manner while the Monkey inspires the Snake to become more outwardly confident. The Monkey values the Snake's advice and opinions and they go through life helping, supporting and encouraging each other. Both are intelligent, sociable, have a good sense of humour and will have many friends. Any children that they have help unite them further.

An excellent match

SNAKE AND ROOSTER

General Relations

These two signs admire each other enormously. They have a good rapport and understanding and general relations between them are good. They enjoy each other's company and delight in the many lively conversations and discussions that they have. Socially the Snake and Rooster can become firm and loyal friends.

These two signs can also form a successful working partnership. The Rooster is the more outgoing and pushy of the two and inspires and motivates the Snake as well as prodding the sometimes over-cautious Snake into action. However, the Rooster gains from the Snake's considerable business acumen and is reassured by the Snake's calm nature. Both signs are ambitious and together can enjoy much success.

In Love and Marriage

The Snake and Rooster are attracted to each other and are well suited.

Unlike some signs, the Snake understands the Rooster well. Behind the Rooster's often blustering exterior there lurks a rich and warm personality and it often takes a quiet and perceptive sign such as the Snake to appreciate the Rooster as he is, rather than as he appears. The Snake delights in his Rooster partner; the Rooster is methodical, a great homemaker, and extremely loyal and faithful – all qualities which are important to the Snake.

Just as the Snake treasures the many virtues of the Rooster, so too the Rooster appreciates the quiet, kind and attentive nature of the Snake. Both signs support and encourage the other and bring out the best in their partner. Admittedly each also has traits the other may dislike – the Rooster's fussiness, the Snake's secrecy – but these are minor hurdles.

An excellent match

SNAKE AND DOG

General Relations

The Snake and Dog both choose their friends with care and it is often some while before either is prepared to lower his reserve and let others into his confidence – and so it is when these two signs meet. Relations are initially cool as they test each other out. But in time the Snake and Dog can develop a good understanding and grow to trust and like each other. The Dog learns to appreciate the Snake's wise and reflective ways, while the Snake admires the Dog's integrity and magnanimous nature.

When the Snake and Dog work together there may be loyalty between them, but not always complete accord. The Snake is ambitious and determined and likes to do things in his own way. The Dog, however, needs to feel motivated before he can give of his best. The Dog is also not as materialistic as the Snake and may be reticent about some of the Snake's actions and motives.

In Love and Marriage

These signs mean much to each other and in love and marriage can find contentment together. However, for this to be so, adjustments need to be made and both need to show a willingness to compromise in times of difficulty.

The Snake is more ambitious and materialistic than the Dog who disapproves of this outlook. The Dog tends to be a worrier and can suffer from bouts of anxiety. While the Snake may sympathize, he may not fully understand the workings of the Dog's mind and may lose patience when the Dog is in one of his darker moods.

Fortunately, both signs are usually able to recognize these problem areas and make every effort to adjust to each other. Also, both possess qualities that the other admires. The Snake values the loyalty and dependability of a Dog partner while the Dog draws comfort from the Snake's calm and confident manner.

A reasonably good match

SNAKE AND PIG

General Relations

The good-natured Pig gets on well with most signs, but the Snake may prove to be the exception. The problem lies in their different personalities. The Pig is honest and open towards others and he expects those he comes in contact with to be the same. However, the Snake can be reserved and secretive and the Pig may find it hard to penetrate the Snake's evasive character. The Pig does not understand the Snake's solitary nature and the Snake feels ill at ease with the Pig's open and easygoing manner.

When the Snake and Pig work together relations between them may also prove tricky. The Pig is far more action orientated than the Snake and the two generally set about their activities in different ways. The Snake is given to much planning and thought, while the Pig prefers to immerse himself straightaway in the action.

In Love and Marriage

Snakes and Pigs have difficulty in relating to each other and in the early stages of any relationship there is some lack of accord. The Pig is puzzled by the Snake's guarded manner, while the Snake finds it hard to open up to the Pig's easygoing and good-humoured nature. A romance between these signs may go through testing moments, but if they are prepared to persist, then it is just possible that they might begin to discover each other's more positive qualities.

In time the Pig learns to recognize the Snake's wisdom. The Snake, in turn, values the trusting nature of the Pig. Under the Pig's influence, the Snake may become more outwardly confident. Both have a fond appreciation of the good things in life and can enjoy a comfortable lifestyle.

However, it should be stressed that a Snake-Pig marriage may not be the easiest and it takes considerable effort and goodwill on both sides for the relationship to work.

A challenging match

THE HORSE

Key characteristics:

Active, alert, outgoing, adventurous, eloquent,
quick tempered.

In love:

To the Horse, love means everything. Passionate,
attentive and faithful.

The Horse is quick witted, has a sharp mind and a wide
range of interests. He has grace, style and elegance and
throughout his life he will put his talents to many uses.
With an adventurous spirit and engaging personality he
makes friends with ease and is often the centre of attention.

The Horse's social life is very important to him and he
will have friends and acquaintances in many walks of life.

The Horse also exudes a strong sex appeal and both male and female Horses never lack admirers. He has a passionate nature and when he is attracted to someone he devotes himself entirely to that person. His whole being is affected and the Horse is totally and utterly in love. The problem is that the Horse tends to fall in and out of love relatively easily and it takes someone special, someone who understands the Horse character well, to retain his affection.

The Horse has many fine qualities and is greatly admired and respected by others. However, the Horse's weaknesses can sometimes undermine his success. Above all, he is restless. He tends to jump from one activity to another and even abandon projects if something else catches his attention. He can also let his enthusiastic nature get the better of him and can act impulsively. The Horse has sparkle, wit and a zest for life and while he may not be the easiest person to live with, life with the Horse is certainly never boring.

Famous Horses

Helena Bonham-Carter, Sean Connery, James Dean, Harrison Ford, Jimi Hendrix, Paul McCartney, Nelson Mandela.

HORSE AND HORSE

General Relations

The Horse enjoys company and he particularly enjoys the company of another Horse. They share many interests and have a similar outlook on life. Their love of conversation leads to some lively and spirited discussions and they spend many a happy hour in each other's company.

In his work the Horse is diligent, enterprising and industrious and by combining their strengths, two Horses can form a strong partnership. They have the drive and enthusiasm to do well. However they should agree on a clear division of responsibilities and remain committed to a specific goal. Without this discipline between them, two Horses may well end up jockeying for control and competing with each other rather than working together.

In Love and Marriage

When the Horse falls in love, he falls truly and deeply in love. There are no half measures. His passion and devotion to the source of his affection is complete. When it is to another lively and spirited Horse, his love knows no bounds. Certainly this is so in the early stages of their relationship.

The Horse has a temper and, although often short lived, many a Horse has said things he has later regretted. When two Horses are together their combined tempers may lead to some heated exchanges. Also, Horses are fiercely independent and without care, this may put strains on their relationship. Fortunately, though, the Horse is well placed to understand another Horse and ideally they will allow each other freedom.

They may have their differences, but they mean much to each other and, with their passionate natures, similar interests and outlooks, their life together can be fulfilling.

A good match

HORSE AND GOAT

General Relations

Although the Horse and Goat have very different personalities they understand each other well. There is an excellent rapport between them and with their lively and sociable natures they enjoy each other's company. They are likely to share many interests, including a love of the countryside, travel and socializing. The Horse and Goat often become close and lasting friends.

The Horse and Goat also work well together. The Goat, who at times can be indecisive, happily leaves much of the decision making to the Horse. The Goat admires the sense of purpose of the Horse, who is content to take the lead. However, should difficulties emerge, the Goat is always at hand to lend support and encourage the Horse. Also, the Horse benefits from the Goat's creativity; he supplies a valuable input of new ideas and suggestions. Their work together will prove successful.

In Love and Marriage

With their lively and sociable natures, the Horse and Goat are often drawn together and in love and marriage are well suited.

The two signs have many interests in common and are likely to lead an active and enjoyable social life. Between them they have a large circle of friends and as a couple they make perfect hosts. The Horse very much values the unfailing and unquestioning support of the Goat and the Goat is an expert at defusing the Horse's temper and boosting his ego. Unlike other signs, the Goat understands the Horse's swings in moods well and is adept at coping with them. The Horse also appreciates the Goat's artistic and creative talents and particularly the Goat's skills as a homemaker.

An excellent match

HORSE AND MONKEY

General Relations

The Horse and Monkey tend to be wary of each other and, while their relations may be reasonable, they are unlikely to become firm friends. The Horse is suspicious of the wily and crafty nature of the Monkey, while the Monkey has problems relating to the strong and independent-minded Horse. General relations between them are never strong.

When the Horse and Monkey are colleagues their combined talents may bring them success. The Horse is industrious and hard working, while the Monkey is enterprising and resourceful. Both are versatile and intelligent and if they are to work together their achievements may be considerable. However, success could be blighted by their mistrust of each other. The honest Horse does not tolerate the sometimes devious ways of the Monkey, while the Monkey is suspicious of the Horse's independent attitude. To attain success they must develop trust in each other.

In Love and Marriage

The Horse and Monkey have many traits in common. They are both strong-minded and outgoing signs. They are versatile, have many interests and set about their activities with verve and enthusiasm. However, they do not relate well to each other and in love and marriage their relationship may not be easy.

The Monkey can be secretive and evasive and is a master at concealing his true feelings, and this is something that irritates the Horse. The Monkey, in turn, is irritated by the Horse's need for independence. Both signs are very strong willed and there will be a constant tussle for authority and the last word.

It takes an exceptional Horse-Monkey couple to make their relationship work, but if they can adjust to each other and allow time to develop individual hobbies, they can remain together as a spirited and lively couple.

A difficult match

HORSE AND ROOSTER

General Relations

Lively, quick witted and sociable, the Horse and Rooster enjoy each other's company. Together they happily attend social functions, have spirited discussions and generally enjoy themselves. For a time they can become good friends, although the long-term prospects may not be so favourable. Both signs can be notoriously candid in their views and their forthright natures can easily get the better of them. When there are things to do and everything is fine, the Horse and Rooster are great chums, but when things start to go wrong, the squabbling starts.

Both the Horse and Rooster are hard workers and, as colleagues, they can enjoy much success. The Horse benefits greatly from the Rooster's organizational skills, while the Rooster gains strength from the Horse's willpower and industry. The main problem is that both are egotistical and both will be keen to take the credit for their achievements.

In Love and Marriage

The Horse and Rooster are often attracted to each other and, with their fine and elegant looks, can make a striking couple. Both are outgoing signs and have many interests in common. For a time the Horse and Rooster can be blissfully happy, but if they are to maintain their affection, they need to show some willingness to adjust to each other.

To find happiness they need to reconcile their different natures. The Horse is more adventurous than the Rooster and likes to do things on the spur of the moment, while the Rooster likes to set about his activities in a more orderly manner. At times the Rooster despairs of the Horse's restlessness, while the Horse finds the Rooster inflexible and set in his ways.

There are undoubtedly problems that the Horse and Rooster face in their relationship but, with their many joint interests and strong physical attraction, they can, with care, still enjoy a lively and fulfilling relationship.

A challenging match

HORSE AND DOG

General Relations

The Horse and Dog understand each other well and can become close companions and lifelong friends. There is respect and trust between them and each does much to help and support the other. They often share similar interests and feel comfortable in each other's company. Generally, relations between the Horse and Dog are excellent.

These two signs also work well together and make a powerful combination. Both work hard and both attach much importance to openness and honesty in their business dealings. Of the two, the Dog may be the more cautious but is a useful restraining influence on some of the Horse's more rash and impulsive notions. However, the enterprising Horse does much to inspire and enthuse the Dog and together, with their individual strengths, they make a successful team.

In Love and Marriage

The Horse and Dog are well suited and in love they can find much happiness. Not only is the physical attraction between them strong but they each have qualities that the other admires. The Horse values the Dog's loving and affectionate ways and draws much strength from his unfailing support.

The Dog, in turn, enjoys the Horse's liveliness, wit and sociable nature. The Horse does much to lift the Dog's spirits and is also able to effectively dispel some of the worries that so often beset the Dog. The Dog recognizes the Horse's need for a certain independence and allows the Horse time to cultivate his own interests.

The Horse and Dog share many interests. They both like to keep themselves active and may have a particular fondness for outdoor activities such as gardening, travelling, and sport.

An excellent match

HORSE AND PIG

General Relations

The Horse and Pig have a high regard for each other and general relations between them are usually good. Both have outgoing and sociable natures and they enjoy each other's company. As friends they lead an active social life and share many interests.

The potential also exists for a good working relationship. The Pig is an astute businessperson and skilful at making money, while the Horse is diligent and hard working. The Horse benefits from the Pig's more persistent manner, while the Pig values the Horse's enthusiasm and enterprise. Their talents and strengths complement each other well, although each needs to remain mindful of the other and it is best if they have a clear division of responsibilities.

In Love and Marriage

The Horse and Pig are often attracted to each other and when in love they can form a close, rewarding relationship. Not only is the physical attraction strong but they understand and relate well to each other.

Both the Horse and Pig have outgoing and lively natures. They like to live life to the full and invariably keep themselves busy with a multitude of interests and an active social life. Both also know how to enjoy themselves and a fair proportion of their time is spent in the agreeable pursuit of pleasure.

These two signs also appreciate each other's talents. The Pig is a good homemaker and the Horse values the comfort and agreeable surroundings that the Pig unfailingly creates. The Pig is both reliable and dependable and can be a useful check on the Horse's restless and impulsive nature. The Pig, in turn, admires the Horse's strength of character and his lively and enterprising nature.

A good match

THE GOAT

Key characteristics:

Creative, artistic, considerate, generous, easygoing, sensitive, a worrier.

In love:

Amorous, affectionate and caring.

Governed by art, the Goat possesses a rich imagination, is creative and prefers the quieter things in life. He has a kindly and caring nature and relates well to others. The Goat hates any sort of discord and quickly shies away from arguments or awkward situations.

In his work the Goat needs an inspiring force behind him. Without this the Goat often lacks the motivation or drive to make the most of his abilities. However, once inspired the Goat can be a diligent and careful worker. He prefers to follow rather than lead and is not a risk-taker. With his artistic skills the Goat excels in any position which enables him to use his creative or imaginative talents.

The Goat has a genial temperament and makes friends easily. Although he may be shy on first meeting someone, once he has got to know that person or feels confident in the group he is with, he can be talkative and witty. He dislikes solitude and endeavours to have others around him.

The female Goat has a caring and considerate nature and is highly regarded by others. She pours much love and energy into her family and home. The male Goat often has a casual appearance and a genial nature. He may not be as assertive or competitive as some, but his charm gets him far.

The Goat often has a large family, but with his easygoing nature he is no disciplinarian and may not cope well with childhood tantrums. However, children respond well to the Goat's kindly nature and Goat parents are able to establish a close and loving bond with their children.

Famous Goats

Jane Austen, Mel Gibson, Michelangelo, Robert de Niro, Rudolph Valentino, Andy Warhol.

GOAT AND GOAT

General Relations

Bright, sociable and often carefree, the Goat enjoys the company of another Goat. Together they have much in common and both are likely to share artistic interests. They also have a fond appreciation for the good life and, providing finances permit, invariably enjoy a fine meal together or attending some lavish function.

In a working situation two Goats can work well together. They trust and respect each other and, if their work is of a creative nature, their joint skills could bring them considerable success. Admittedly the Goat is not the most commercially minded of signs, but in a working situation Goats support and inspire each other and can do well. However, as both can be indulgent, they must exercise discipline when dealing with the financial aspects of any concern.

In Love and Marriage

The Goat is an amorous, passionate and sensual sign and the attraction between two Goats is strong. Both know how to enjoy themselves and have an appreciation of the finer things in life.

Goats are superb homemakers and their home is a veritable lovenest. Between them they pour much energy into creating and setting up their home and both regard it as their own private and secure sanctuary – a protection from the outside world.

However, problems can arise. The Goat tends to spend his money freely, and when two Goats are together there may be little control over the purse strings. Also, when problems arise, the Goat can be a pessimist and when two Goats are downhearted they may have difficulty in lifting each other's spirits. Fortunately, though, many Goat couples are quick to detect problem areas, and as neither likes unpleasantness, difficulties that arise are quickly swept aside.

A well matched couple

GOAT AND MONKEY

General Relations

The Goat and Monkey enjoy each other's company and relations between them can be good. Both are outgoing and sociable signs and find each other interesting and congenial company. They respect and like each other and can become firm friends.

In a working situation the Goat and Monkey can get on well together. The Monkey appreciates the creative and inventive talents of the Goat, while the Goat recognizes the resourcefulness and enterprise of the Monkey. The Monkey does much to motivate the Goat and, when united in pursuing a specific goal, their original and enterprising ways can lead them to success. There is a good level of respect and trust between them, although the more security-conscious Goat may not be as much of a risk taker as the Monkey.

In Love and Marriage

Goats and Monkeys are often attracted to each other and their relationship is full of fun, variety and lots of love. Their witty and inventive natures keep each other amused and there is much affection between them.

The Goat and Monkey value each other's strengths. The Monkey appreciates the Goat's talents as a homemaker as well as his artistic and creative skills. The Monkey understands the Goat well and does much to help and encourage him.

Similarly, the Goat admires – and is comforted by – the resourcefulness of the Monkey. Whenever there is a problem the Monkey is there with a solution. However, it is possible that the Goat may become increasingly dependent upon the Monkey and if this becomes too much of a restraint he may become resentful and problems could emerge. Also, the Goat is much more romantic and sensitive than the Monkey.

Generally, however, the Goat and Monkey mean much to each other and any difficulties can be reconciled.

A good match

GOAT AND ROOSTER

General Relations

The Goat and Rooster have very different personalities and viewpoints and relations between them can prove difficult. The Rooster is efficient, methodical and practical, while the Goat has a much more easygoing and carefree nature. The Rooster is candid and forthright and the Goat is wary of his matter-of-fact tones.

Their different outlooks also pose problems at work. The Rooster is a hard worker, given to much planning and organization. The Goat, however, lacks discipline and often needs motivation and encouragement. The Rooster views the laid-back attitude of the Goat with disdain, while the Goat regards the Rooster's attitude as overbearing and pedantic. The only salvation is if their business is of a creative nature and the Rooster is able to manage the affairs of the Goat.

In Love and Marriage

The Goat and Rooster do not have much in common and have to make major adjustments if they are to enjoy a close and harmonious relationship. The Rooster is well organized and given to planning his activities with care. The Goat, however, has a much more relaxed attitude to life.

The Goat is also more sensitive than the Rooster and all too often the Goat's feelings are upset by the Rooster's candid remarks. Similarly, the Rooster finds it hard to relate to the Goat's sometimes whimsical and fanciful nature and often despairs of his capriciousness.

A lasting and harmonious relationship between these so very different signs can prove a challenge for both. But if the Goat and Rooster's love for each other is strong enough then it is possible that they may make the adjustments needed to make their relationship work.

A difficult match

GOAT AND DOG

General Relations

There is little affinity between the Goat and Dog. They have few interests in common and their different personalities rarely gel. The capricious and whimsical Goat finds little favour with the more serious and dutiful Dog, while the Goat finds the Dog cynical, stubborn and idealistic.

This lack of accord is also apparent when the Goat and Dog are colleagues. To do well, both signs need encouragement and motivation, and this is something neither is able to provide for the other. The Dog is distrustful of the Goat's laid-back manner, while the Goat may find it hard to come to terms with the Dog's idealistic attitudes. Neither is commercially minded and, as both can be worriers, should they encounter problems they are more likely to drown in a sea of anxiety than plan for survival. They may well prefer to go their separate ways rather than struggle on together.

In Love and Marriage

Between them the Goat and Dog have many fine qualities. The Goat is kindly and good natured, while the Dog is loyal and attentive. But these signs also have weaknesses and when the Goat and Dog come together they seem to accentuate their negative traits.

The problem stems from their different personalities and outlooks. The Dog is an idealist and ever mindful of his duties and responsibilities. He can also be stubborn, obstinate and forthright. The Goat can be sensitive to the Dog's criticism and seeks a more active and lively existence than the Dog can provide.

The Dog in turn has little appreciation of the Goat's imaginative nature and does not tolerate the Goat's whimsy. The Dog is direct, practical and matter of fact and the Goat is not. It takes a very special Goat-Dog couple to make a relationship work.

A difficult match

GOAT AND PIG

General Relations

The Goat and Pig are lively, sociable and good-natured signs and can get on well together. Not only do they enjoy an active social life, but their different personalities prove complementary. The Goat feels at ease and secure with the genial yet robust Pig, while the Pig enjoys the Goat's easy-going nature. They can strike up a good rapport and often become firm and trusted friends.

The Goat and Pig also work well together. The Goat benefits from the commercial acumen and money-making talents of the Pig, while the Pig values the Goat's imagination and creative skills. In such a partnership the Goat often provides the ideas, while the Pig has the drive and expertise to put the ideas into practice. They help, motivate and inspire each other and again there is good rapport and trust between them.

In Love and Marriage

The Goat and Pig both have amorous and sensual natures and often fall for each other. There is a great physical attraction between them and their sex life is active and fulfilling. Their personalities are also highly compatible. Both have placid temperaments and aim for a harmonious and stress-free existence.

The Goat – who seeks a resourceful and loving mate – is certainly not disappointed by the Pig. The Pig not only makes him feel secure but does much to ease his many worries. He even tolerates the Goat's capriciousness.

The Pig, in turn, not only values the support and affection of the Goat, but also his expert skills as a homemaker. Between them they put much effort into their home and help each other with their various activities. They have a large number of friends and as a couple make perfect hosts.

An excellent match

THE MONKEY

Key characteristics:

Resourceful, charming, persuasive, amusing,
sociable, cunning.

In love:

Captivating and knows how to impress!

The monkey entertains and intrigues and those born under
the Monkey sign are similarly skilled at capturing our
attention and winning our approval. The Monkey is governed by fantasy and has a delightful sense of humour and
persuasive personality.

The Monkey can do well in almost any line of work.
However, he is at his best when facing challenges or has
some objective to meet. He soon becomes bored with

routine or mundane tasks. He can lack persistence; if he feels a goal is not within immediate reach, his interest can soon wane. The Monkey is action oriented and is more interested in the present and the near future than the years to come.

Having such an engaging manner the Monkey is popular with the opposite sex, but affairs of the heart do not always run smoothly. Even though he may appear cheery and outgoing on the outside, he is adept at hiding his true feelings and emotions. This can cause him emotional turmoil.

The Monkey truly delights in parenthood, particularly as it gives him the chance to rekindle the joys of his childhood years. The Monkey often remains young at heart.

The female Monkey has a lively and vivacious nature. Like her male counterpart, she is inquisitive and extremely versatile. She has a persuasive manner and likes to lead an active social life. The male Monkey, too, likes to impress others – he invariably succeeds.

Famous Monkeys

Julius Caesar, Bette Davis, Michael Douglas, Mia Farrow, Tom Hanks, Peter O'Toole, Leonardo da Vinci.

MONKEY AND MONKEY

General Relations

With such a friendly and personable nature, the Monkey makes friends with considerable ease and who better to win his admiration and friendship than another sociable Monkey? Monkeys get on famously well with each other and general relations between them are usually excellent. Together they become accomplices, spurring and encouraging each other on to better and greater things.

In business few doubt the Monkey's flair and ability. However, when two Monkeys work together a certain discipline is needed to make the relationship succeed. For all his many talents, the Monkey has an extremely competitive streak and often strives to go one better than the rest – and this includes trying to outwit another Monkey! If both Monkeys can resist the temptation to get the better of their partner then their combined strengths may bring them much success.

In Love and Marriage

There is a strong attraction between two Monkeys and, in love and marriage, they enjoy a happy, harmonious and close relationship.

Monkeys understand each other well and can build up a good rapport. They have many interests, some of which they share, but some that they happily continue on their own. Monkeys also recognize a need for freedom in their relationship and this they allow each other.

Monkeys also like to keep themselves active and their life together is full of variety, new challenges and lots of fun. They like socializing, enjoy travelling and have a thirst for adventure and there is always something going on – life is never dull in a Monkey household!

The Monkey couple also take great pride in any children they have and make loving and caring parents. Monkeys enjoy parenthood and between them devote much time and energy to their children.

A splendid match

MONKEY AND ROOSTER

General Relations

The Monkey and Rooster are two forceful and outgoing signs and generally do not get on well together. The Monkey is a lively and high-spirited individual who likes to retain a certain amount of freedom in his actions, while the Rooster is more disciplined and much more conservative in outlook. The Rooster views the Monkey as an impetuous and undisciplined character, while the Monkey has little time for the Rooster's pedantic ways or forthright nature.

This lack of rapport is also evident when the Monkey and Rooster work together. Their approach to their work is often very different. The methodical and efficient Rooster likes to plan and organize his activities, while the Monkey is more of an opportunist and relies a lot on his charm and wits. There is little trust between them and unless they can unite in a common purpose, they quickly go their separate ways.

In Love and Marriage

With their outgoing and sociable natures, the Monkey and Rooster may be drawn together. The Rooster finds the Monkey lively and fascinating company, while the Monkey appreciates the style and self-assuredness of the Rooster. For a time they may get on well, particularly as both like partying and socializing. But their love and admiration for each other may be hard to maintain and in love and marriage the outlook may be bleak.

The problem lies in their very different natures. The Monkey is quick witted and resourceful and likes independence. The Rooster, however, is a great planner and organizer – not only of his own activities but of those around him. The Monkey is more action oriented and more spontaneous than the Rooster and he may find the Rooster a restraining influence. Nor does he care for the Rooster's forthright and candid manner. The Rooster, in turn, will be irritated by the Monkey's crafty nature and also consider him too materialistic in outlook.

A difficult match

MONKEY AND DOG

General Relations

There are many differences in outlook between the Monkey and Dog and, on a casual basis, relations between them may prove difficult. The altruistic Dog does not care for the self-seeking and opportunistic ways of the Monkey, while the Monkey finds the Dog too idealistic and unyielding for his liking. However, if each is prepared to get to know the other better, then they begin to appreciate each other's finer qualities and relations between them improve.

When the Monkey and Dog work together they benefit from each other's strengths. The Monkey is more enterprising and commercially minded than the Dog, while the Dog tends to be more disciplined and persistent than the Monkey. If they can unite in pursuing a specific goal, then the Monkey and Dog can enjoy much success, although the more honourable Dog may not be too keen on some of the Monkey's more crafty ploys.

In Love and Marriage

While initial relations between the Monkey and Dog may be reserved, the closer they draw together the better they appreciate each other's personality.

Each benefits from the qualities found in the other and in many respects their different strengths compensate for the weaknesses in the other. The more lively and spirited Monkey does much to alleviate some of the worries that beset the anxious Dog. The Dog also benefits from the Monkey's lively and sociable nature. Under the Monkey's influence he becomes more relaxed and outgoing.

The Monkey also gains from the Dog. The Dog is sincere, well meaning and thoughtful and the Monkey values the Dog's judgement. His strong ethical standing rubs off on the Monkey and he becomes more open and honourable in his dealings. If the Monkey and Dog have a family, this unites them further and both make proud and attentive parents.

A good match

MONKEY AND PIG

General Relations

The Monkey and Pig are both lively, outgoing and sociable signs and can get on extremely well together. There is a good understanding and rapport between them and they can become firm friends. They learn much from each other and both the Monkey and the Pig also tend to bring out the better qualities in the other.

The Monkey and Pig also work well together. Both recognize and value each other's strengths and there is co-operation and trust between them. The Monkey values the Pig's ability to work hard and his money-making talents, while the Pig draws strength and inspiration from the zest and enterprise of the Monkey. Also, under the Pig's watchful eye, the Monkey is prevented from carrying out some of his more crafty notions. While the Monkey is not above duping others, the Monkey holds the Pig in too high a regard to trick his porcine partner.

In Love and Marriage

With their warm, friendly and sociable natures, the Monkey and Pig are often attracted to each other and can form a loving and harmonious relationship.

Together they cultivate their joint interests and, with their multitude of friends, enjoy an active social life. The Monkey readily appreciates the Pig's skills as a homemaker as well as delighting in the Pig's genial disposition. The Pig feels inspired by the enthusiasm of the Monkey, while the Monkey is reassured by the love and loyalty of the Pig. Each does much to support and encourage the other.

The more honourable Pig may, however, disapprove of the Monkey's more scheming and opportunistic ways, but under the Pig's influence the Monkey may well change for the better and become more open in his dealings and outlook. The Monkey may also become less self-centred. Similarly, the Monkey is a good adviser for the sometimes naïve Pig.

An excellent match

THE ROOSTER

Key characteristics:

Meticulous, efficient, orderly, conscientious, intelligent, honourable, notoriously candid.

In love:

Sincere, caring and loyal.

The rooster commands attention, is orderly and vigilant and so, too, are many who are born under the tenth Chinese sign.

In his manner the Rooster appears confident and self-assured. He is often given to flamboyant gestures and he likes to be in the limelight. He is sincere, honourable and trusting and can be fascinating company. The Rooster likes to lead an active social life. Extremely well-organized, it is sometimes remarkable just what he can cram into a day.

Keenly intelligent, with a sharp mind and a good memory, the Rooster does well in his chosen career. He is an adept and powerful speaker, but can be extremely candid in expressing his views. Some admire his honestly, but others regard him as inconsiderate and abrasive.

Underneath all the flamboyance there exists someone who is not always as confident as he first appears; a person who is anxious to please. It takes someone special to penetrate the barriers that he sets up around himself. Although he may seem outgoing and highly sociable, he is in fact an intensely private person.

The female Rooster, the Hen, is highly conscientious and thorough in all she does. In her work, the upbringing of her children or the upkeep of her home, she sets herself high standards and aims to please. The male Rooster likes to impress and tends to wear distinctive clothes.

Famous Roosters

Michael Caine, Dawn French, Goldie Hawn, D. H. Lawrence, Michelle Pfeiffer, Roman Polanski.

ROOSTER AND ROOSTER

General Relations

The Rooster is a lively and proud individual who picks his friends with care. While he may recognize many of his own qualities in another Rooster, his forceful and domineering nature gets the better of him and prevents two Roosters from ever becoming close or lasting friends. The Rooster likes to be in charge and have his own way and such an attitude leads to conflicts with another equally strong-minded Rooster.

When two Roosters are colleagues or business partners again difficulties arise. Each wants to organize and command the other. Neither gives way easily and rather than working together they are more likely to end up competing against each other.

In Love and Marriage

Roosters have many admirable qualities but when two Roosters get together their personalities clash and, rather than bringing out the positive qualities in each other, they invariably end up squabbling and competing with each other. Neither finds compromise easy and each tries to get the upper hand. The Rooster has an extremely competitive streak and feels that only one can rule the roost.

There are, of course, exceptions to the norm and it is just possible that two Roosters may make a success of their relationship. Ideally they should agree on a specific division of responsibilities but at the same time cultivate their joint interests. However as both will speak their minds openly and forcefully, arguments are likely to occur even in the best of situations.

A difficult match

ROOSTER AND DOG

General Relations

These two signs are both strong willed and strong minded and generally do not get on well together. Both have traits that irritate the other and as both can be forthright in expressing their views, tempers readily fly. The Rooster dislikes the Dog's stubbornness and cynical nature, while the Dog finds the Rooster vain and egotistical.

In business their different outlooks again pose problems. For the Dog to realize his true potential he needs to feel inspired and motivated – and the Rooster is more likely to alienate him than win his trust. The Rooster's forceful manner and methodical nature make him feel ill at ease. The Rooster, in turn, may feel unnerved by the worrying and anxious nature of the Dog. When problems emerge their forthright natures get the better of them and their partnership degenerates into arguments and bitter recrimination.

In Love and Marriage

The Rooster and Dog have very different personalities – and while for some signs personality differences can prove complementary, this is not always the case with these two signs. Their differences lead to conflict and should the Rooster and Dog fall in love and decide to marry, their relationship may be fraught with difficulties.

Part of the problem lies in their opposing outlooks. The Rooster can be vain, opinionated and self-centred, while the Dog is more altruistic and disapproves of the egocentricity of the Rooster. Also the Rooster has a tendency to dominate and to impose his sense of order upon others and the strong-minded Dog resents this. While the Dog does not like being bossed around and he may feel that the Rooster, with his flamboyant and exuberant style, goes over the top, is over-fussy and too interfering. Both can be forthright in expressing their views and arguments may be a frequent occurrence.

A difficult match

ROOSTER AND PIG

General Relations

The amiable and affable Pig gets on well with most and, while the Pig may dislike the egocentricity of the Rooster, he nevertheless has a sneaking admiration for the resolute and candid bird. Similarly, the Rooster warms to the genial and trusting disposition of the Pig and general relations between them are good, although not necessarily close.

In business both the Rooster and Pig are hard working and if they are united in pursuing a specific goal they can make an effective combination. However, the more cautious Rooster may not feel totally at ease with some of the risks that the Pig takes, while the Pig may at times find the Rooster's attitude inflexible and restrictive. Both are honourable in their business dealings and, even though they may not always be in full agreement with each other, there is a good level of respect between them.

In Love and Marriage

There is much attraction between the Rooster and Pig and, while the early days of their romance may not be smooth (both signs need time to adjust to each other) the longer their relationship continues, the better it becomes.

The Pig is much more easygoing and tolerant than the Rooster and falls in with many of the plans and routines that the Rooster imposes upon his household. The Rooster is a greater organizer and having such an efficient partner may be of assistance to the Pig. Similarly, under the Pig's good-natured influence, the Rooster may become more reserved and lose his inhibitions.

As a couple these two signs are likely to have several interests in common. Both pour much time and energy into their home and may also share an interest in gardening. They are keen socializers and between them have many friends.

A beneficial match

THE DOG

Key characteristics:

Honest, dependable, diligent, perceptive, selfless, caring, pessimistic.

In love:

Very loyal and dutiful but keenly aware of the feelings of others.

Whether as a pet, a farm dog, or protector of property, the dog has long been regarded as man's best friend. Many of the noble features of the dog can be found in those born under this sign.

Governed by loyalty and anxiety, the Dog has a dutiful and responsible manner. A good judge of character, he takes his time forming friendships and is much admired for his sincerity, good nature and integrity. The Dog inspires confidence and trust. Although he may not be as ambitious as some other signs, he is often elevated to positions of authority simply because he has earned the trust and confidence of others. Of all the Chinese signs, the Dog is one of the most selfless.

He has a sociable nature and is invariably popular and well liked. He much prefers small gatherings to large parties and when he is in company of friends he can shine. Around strangers he can become introverted and morose.

The female Dog tends to be more outgoing than the male. She has a charming manner, converses well and is a good judge of character. She sets about her activities in a responsible and diligent way and is greatly loved by her family and friends.

The Dog makes a fine and dutiful parent. He devotes much time and attention to his children although, in view of his anxious nature, he can be prone to worry unduly over them.

Famous Dogs:

Brigitte Bardot, Michael Jackson, Madonna, Elvis Presley, Mother Teresa, Prince William.

DOG AND DOG

General Relations

There is much camaraderie between two Dogs and general relations between them are good. Dogs trust and under-stand each other and have similar outlooks and views. There is also considerable co-operation between them and they do much to help and support each other.

When Dogs work together there is trust and respect between them but this does not necessarily lead to success. The Dog tends to be a worrier and when difficult decisions need to be taken, the Dog couple may be fraught with anx-iety and tension. To do well the Dog needs a resolute figure alongside him who can provide inspiration and motivation. If they are lucky, a Dog team could just possibly make it – especially if their work is of a humanitarian nature and material goals are not so important – but, generally, a work-ing relationship between two Dogs may not be the best.

In Love and Marriage

Dogs are romantics and when two Dogs fall in love there is a great meeting of minds and hearts. A Dog devotes himself completely to his partner and in a relationship between two Dogs there is much love, trust and understanding.

As a couple they do much to help and encourage each other. They work as a team and their loyalty and devotion to each other is unquestioned. Together they cultivate joint interests and, with their practical natures, often content themselves in carrying out projects around their home and garden. They make caring and attentive parents.

With their dutiful and serious natures there may not be an abundance of mirth in a Dog household, and as both are outspoken arguments may well occur. However, Dogs are resilient and together they will ride out any storms.

A devoted couple

DOG AND PIG

General Relations

The Dog and Pig admire and respect each other and can become good and lasting friends. The Pig is attracted by the Dog's loyal and unselfish nature, while the Dog likes the Pig's genial, kindly and sincere manner. There is considerable rapport and understanding between them and general relations between these two signs are invariably good.

These two signs also work well together. Both are open and honourable in their business dealings and the Dog draws inspiration from the hard-working Pig. The Pig is the more enterprising of the two, but can also be gullible and the Dog does much to protect and support his partner and friend. The Dog may not be as materialistic or so profit driven as the Pig but there is still much respect and trust between them.

In Love and Marriage

There is much respect and understanding between the Dog and Pig and in love and marriage they are well suited.

The warm-hearted Pig values the loyalty and sincerity of the Dog, while the Dog enjoys the easygoing company of the Pig. The Pig's genial temperament is a good antidote for some of the worries that beset the Dog. Similarly, the Pig values the dependability of the Dog and pays heed to the Dog's wise counsel. Both make caring and loving parents and any children will have a wonderful upbringing.

As in most relationships there are problems they need to address. Both can be stubborn and obstinate. The Dog may find the Pig over-indulgent and sometimes lacking in refinement, while the Pig may not care for the Dog's outspoken and cynical views.

Fortunately none of these problems are insurmountable and both value their relationship enough to adjust to the other.

A splendid match

THE PIG

Key characteristics:

Sincere, honest, trusting, sociable, hard working, stubborn.

In love:

Passionate, sensual and loyal.

Those born under the twelfth and final Chinese sign have many fine virtues. The Pig is sincere, trusting and relates very well to others. He has a genial nature and people feel at ease in his company. He enjoys socializing and has a fondness for the good things in life. He likes wining and dining and is often a keen partygoer.

Although the Pig may not be as competitive as some signs, he is diligent and persevering and his loyalty and integrity is much appreciated by his employers. However, it sometimes takes him a little while – and several false starts – before he decides what he really wants to do and finds where his talents really lie.

In matters of the heart the Pig is sensuous and passionate. In his youth he can be promiscuous and flirtatious and throws himself fully into his relationships. However, once he settles down he will be loyal and faithful and makes a fine and caring spouse. His home life is most important to him and he strives to give his home a calm and harmonious atmosphere.

The female Pig has a particularly lively and engaging manner. She is sociable, sincere and trusting. She is attentive to her partner and her children and devotes herself unselfishly to their needs – often at the cost of her career. The male Pig has an agreeable and amiable manner and is well liked, but underneath his genial nature, the male Pig also possesses a stubborn streak and can be quite obstinate at times.

Famous Pigs

Woody Allen, Humphrey Bogart, Glenn Close, Pete Sampras, Steven Spielberg, Emma Thompson.

PIG AND PIG

General Relations

The warm, friendly and sociable Pig is one sign who knows how to enjoy himself and when two Pigs get together they can be assured of having a great time. Two Pigs together make good friends and fine companions and general relations between them are excellent. They also do much to help and support each other and invariably share the same views and outlooks.

Two Pigs also work well together. The Pig is usually lucky in business and an astute money-maker and, when two Pigs combine their talents, success is also certainly assured. Pigs are hard and honest workers and through sheer determination and willpower they are determined to secure their objectives and make the most of their talents. There is trust and understanding between them and in business they make an excellent combination.

In Love and Marriage

Kindly, sociable and reliable, the Pig makes an ideal partner and two Pigs together can find much happiness and contentment.

Pigs understand each other well, they support and encourage each other and bring out their positive qualities. The Pig often needs an understanding and encouraging partner to help him realize his potential and who better to appreciate this than another Pig?

A Pig couple will devote much time and energy to setting up and maintaining their home. Pigs are very much home-loving creatures and invariably fit their home with all the latest in comforts as well as giving it a stable and harmonious atmosphere.

Pigs also know how to enjoy themselves and a Pig couple leads an active social life, has many friends and a wide range of interests. They enjoy dining, partying and, with their passionate and sensual natures, enjoy an active sex life. A Pig couple live and enjoy life to the full!

An excellent match

THE CHINESE YEARS

Rat	31 January 1900	to	18 February 1901
Ox	19 February 1901	to	7 February 1902
Tiger	8 February 1902	to	28 January 1903
Rabbit	29 January 1903	to	15 February 1904
Dragon	16 February 1904	to	3 February 1905
Snake	4 February 1905	to	24 January 1906
Horse	25 January 1906	to	12 February 1907
Goat	13 February 1907	to	1 February 1908
Monkey	2 February 1908	to	21 January 1909
Rooster	22 January 1909	to	9 February 1910
Dog	10 February 1910	to	29 January 1911
Pig	30 January 1911	to	17 February 1912
Rat	18 February 1912	to	5 February 1913
Ox	6 February 1913	to	25 January 1914
Tiger	26 January 1914	to	13 February 1915
Rabbit	14 February 1915	to	2 February 1916
Dragon	3 February 1916	to	22 January 1917

Snake	23 January 1917	to	10 February 1918
Horse	11 February 1918	to	31 January 1919
Goat	1 February 1919	to	19 February 1920
Monkey	20 February 1920	to	7 February 1921
Rooster	8 February 1921	to	27 January 1922
Dog	28 January 1922	to	15 February 1923
Pig	16 February 1923	to	4 February 1924
Rat	5 February 1924	to	23 January 1925
Ox	24 January 1925	to	12 February 1926
Tiger	13 February 1926	to	1 February 1927
Rabbit	2 February 1927	to	22 January 1928
Dragon	23 January 1928	to	9 February 1929
Snake	10 February 1929	to	29 January 1930
Horse	30 January 1930	to	16 February 1931
Goat	17 February 1931	to	5 February 1932
Monkey	6 February 1932	to	25 January 1933
Rooster	26 January 1933	to	13 February 1934
Dog	14 February 1934	to	3 February 1935
Pig	4 February 1935	to	23 January 1936
Rat	24 January 1936	to	10 February 1937
Ox	11 February 1937	to	30 January 1938
Tiger	31 January 1938	to	18 February 1939
Rabbit	19 February 1939	to	7 February 1940
Dragon	8 February 1940	to	26 January 1941

Snake	27 January 1941	to	14 February 1942
Horse	15 February 1942	to	4 February 1943
Goat	5 February 1943	to	24 January 1944
Monkey	25 January 1944	to	12 February 1945
Rooster	13 February 1945	to	1 February 1946
Dog	2 February 1946	to	21 January 1947
Pig	22 January 1947	to	9 February 1948
Rat	10 February 1948	to	28 January 1949
Ox	29 January 1949	to	16 February 1950
Tiger	17 February 1950	to	5 February 1951
Rabbit	6 February 1951	to	26 January 1952
Dragon	27 January 1952	to	13 February 1953
Snake	14 February 1953	to	2 February 1954
Horse	3 February 1954	to	23 January 1955
Goat	24 January 1955	to	11 February 1956
Monkey	12 February 1956	to	30 January 1957
Rooster	31 January 1957	to	17 February 1958
Dog	18 February 1958	to	7 February 1959
Pig	8 February 1959	to	27 January 1960
Rat	28 January 1960	to	14 February 1961
Ox	15 February 1961	to	4 February 1962
Tiger	5 February 1962	to	24 January 1963
Rabbit	25 January 1963	to	12 February 1964
Dragon	13 February 1964	to	1 February 1965

Snake	2 February 1965	to	20 January 1966
Horse	21 January 1966	to	8 February 1967
Goat	9 February 1967	to	29 January 1968
Monkey	30 January 1968	to	16 February 1969
Rooster	17 February 1969	to	5 February 1970
Dog	6 February 1970	to	26 January 1971
Pig	27 January 1971	to	14 February 1972
Rat	15 February 1972	to	2 February 1973
Ox	3 February 1973	to	22 January 1974
Tiger	23 January 1974	to	10 February 1975
Rabbit	11 February 1975	to	30 January 1976
Dragon	31 January 1976	to	17 February 1977
Snake	18 February 1977	to	6 February 1978
Horse	7 February 1978	to	27 January 1979
Goat	28 January 1979	to	15 February 1980
Monkey	16 February 1980	to	4 February 1981
Rooster	5 February 1981	to	24 January 1982
Dog	25 January 1982	to	12 February 1983
Pig	13 February 1983	to	1 February 1984
Rat	2 February 1984	to	19 February 1985
Ox	20 February 1985	to	8 February 1986
Tiger	9 February 1986	to	28 January 1987
Rabbit	29 January 1987	to	16 February 1988
Dragon	17 February 1988	to	5 February 1989

Snake	6 February 1989	to	26 January 1990
Horse	27 January 1990	to	14 February 1991
Goat	15 February 1991	to	3 February 1992
Monkey	4 February 1992	to	22 January 1993
Rooster	23 January 1993	to	9 February 1994
Dog	10 February 1994	to	30 January 1995
Pig	31 January 1995	to	18 February 1996
Rat	19 February 1996	to	6 February 1997
Ox	7 February 1997	to	27 January 1998
Tiger	28 January 1998	to	15 February 1999
Rabbit	16 February 1999	to	4 February 2000